D0391677

THE KIDS ARE ALRIGHT

THE KIDS ARE ALRIGHT

HOW THE GAMER GENERATION
IS CHANGING THE WORKPLACE

John C. Beck
Mitchell Wade

HARVARD BUSINESS SCHOOL PRESS
BOSTON, MASSACHUSETTS

978-1-4221-0435-4 (ISBN 13)

Library of Congress Cataloging-in-Publication Data forthcoming.

Contents

Acknowledgments

Perhaps it's natural that, in a book with two authors, the many people who deserve acknowledgment also fall into groups of two. Both of us are grateful to:

Over two thousand very important people we have never met: all those who took the time to complete our long and detailed questionnaire. Together, these business professionals provided the very first data showing a direct, statistically verifiable link between all those digital games that Americans play growing up and the changing professional behavior we see around us. We couldn't have done this research without them—and, thanks to them, we'll never look at games in the same way again.

Roughly two hundred people we did meet—the ones who were generous enough to provide rich detail from their personal and professional experience, so that we could bring those statistics to life. Enthusiastic gamers and worried parents, industry insiders and unabashed critics, interview subjects and working colleagues—each of these groups helped us understand this new world, and how it connects to our own.[1] We are particularly grateful to our consulting clients, who kept our thinking about the game generation grounded in the problems that real managers and executives face right now.

Two pairs of people who pushed the edges of some very important envelopes. The first pair, George Arquilla and Roger Beck, went far beyond the standard expectations of research assistants; instead, they always found exactly the data, contact, or material we needed, exactly when we needed it, even when what we needed wasn't exactly what we asked for. The second pair, Jacqueline Murphy and Astrid Sandoval of Harvard Business School Press, pushed this book to be much more than it would have been without them. We are grateful not only for their professional skill, but for their personal commitment. Jacque, who was there at the creation, saw the promise of this subject when it was far from obvious.

Finally, we are grateful to two people whom we view not only as valued colleagues, but as real partners in this research. Patrick Lynch made sure that the survey design, methods, and analysis were sound, sophisticated, and smart. He is unmatched at his craft. He is also the kind of serious scholar who brings surprise, humor, and pure randomness to any team meeting. Adam Carstens joined the project later, in theory just to supplement our research. While he is indeed the fastest and most flexible person we have ever seen at finding data on the Web, that may be the least of his contributions to the book. His insights, challenges, and turns of phrase are everywhere. We are delighted that fate has brought us these two thought partners, and we can't wait for the next project that brings us all together.

We extend our thanks to all of these people. Much of the information that follows was originally theirs. The mistakes, of course, are ours.

Preface

When this book on the real-world impact of videogames was first published, we were surprised by the response. We had originally written it with business in mind—after all, we had just discovered the first hard data on how the gamer generation was prepared to be employees and executives.

Yet it turned out that business was just a small part of the story. After every speech, we were approached by parent after concerned parent thanking us for giving them hope that their kids might be alright. Ever since they were invented, videogames have scared parents. As the games get more powerful, parents get more scared.

It's easy to see why. Videogames have replaced television as kids' favorite babysitter. But they are much more insidious. They get into our brains. TV is about watching; games are about doing. And doing is where we learn.

Even as adults, we learn only about 10 percent of what we watch, but over 70 percent of what we do. And in the formative years, learning from games may be even more powerful. Psychologists tell us that the basic neural pathways of the brain are formed up to about age fifteen. (That's why kids learn languages so easily.)

So parents should be concerned; videogames are hard-wiring our kids' brains. What are they putting in there?

We're both parents ourselves. And we're not really gamers. So we began this research with plenty of worries, and some prejudice, too. Sure, we thought, gamers might have better reflexes, or a stronger competitive drive. But after thousands of hours immersed in fantasy worlds, could they handle reality?

What we found shocked us. First, there is a lot of good news. The ninety million kids who grew up gaming are more social, more loyal to their teams, more sophisticated decision makers than their counterparts who didn't play video games in their formative years. Who would have thought? But the even bigger surprise to us as fathers was this: this generation is literally growing up in the world of videogames. That world is completely different from the one all of us grew up in. And growing up there is making this generation—our kids—visibly, measurably different.

They can handle reality, all right—in some ways even better than we do. All those hours spent playing video games are actually teaching them important skills. But they don't see things the way nongamers do, and they don't maneuver the same way. For their great new skills to work in our nongamer world, they need some help adapting.

That's important news for managers. It's even more important for parents. And for both, the vital message is the same:

- We can actually understand the strange world in which kids are growing up.

- We can see the specific, predictable ways that our kids don't fit the baby boom world of schools and colleges and teams and jobs—all still run by nongamers.
- We can each help kids turn what they have learned in all those hours of gaming into an asset in the real world.
- And we don't have to spend hundreds of hours playing videogames to do it.

When you review the data from our national survey; when you listen to gamers, parents, teachers, and bosses like the hundreds interviewed for this book; when you take a look inside the strange world of videogames, the patterns become clear. You can do a lot more than just worry. There are clear challenges, and clear opportunities. (For a sample, take a look at the box "7 Habits of Highly Typical Gamers.")

Even better, you can relax. The kids really *are* alright. And they can be fantastic. They've got a lot to add—believe us, we've seen the data. The trick is for us nongamers to see it, and then to help them connect. That's what this book is all about.

MW

JCB

7 HABITS OF HIGHLY TYPICAL GAMERS

The Kids Are Alright teaches seven principles. Some can work in the rest of the world; some can't. But start from here, and you can help young people really contribute to the world beyond Playstation.

1. Everyone Can Succeed.
Gamers grow up in a world where literally everyone can succeed at just about anything. By working hard enough (and long enough), it is possible for every player to win these games. While John's son with Down Syndrome takes longer to get through all the levels in a game of Tony Hawk, he can do it. That experience gives these young people great courage, ambition, and persistence. The trick is to keep the "game" interesting, challenging, and fun—and to help each "player" see where extra investment of time and effort just isn't possible.

2. You Gotta Play the Odds.
This generation grows up playing games of chance. There has been a probability algorithm built into almost every game they've played. Our survey found that gamers are twice as likely as boomers to believe success in life is due to luck. This prepares them to shrug off pretty serious setbacks (remember the dot-com bust?) as learning experiences in which their luck just ran out. It also teaches them to analyze the game they are playing and—if the odds don't seem good—to look elsewhere. Of course, there are times in life—falling in love? Choosing a career?—when "the odds" just aren't what's important. A little coaching could help.

3. Learn from the Team, Not the Coach.

But that coaching will have to be subtle. With this generation, your high school coach probably won't cut it. Gamers are surprisingly good at teamwork. They love working together and helping each other. They often game in groups. Even the youngest are encouraged to learn new skills, because the game stays most interesting when everyone in the room has competitive ability. But they're much less used to learning from their elders. We baby boomers grew up with adult coaches telling us to bunt or swing, run or hold up, hold the ball or throw. Each child was a competitor for the coach's attention. In the world of video games, though, there is usually no adult present. And no gamers "practice" before they play video games; they learn by doing, together. So, whenever you can, resist the urge to dint; often you "teach" better by introducing a group of gamers to a problem and then just getting out of the way.

4. Kill Bosses, Trust Strategy Guides.

This whole generation knows that the "boss" is to be at least ignored, but, in many cases, destroyed. In video games, the "Level Boss" is the hardest obstacle to get past to achieve your goal. So gamers can have—um, issues—with traditional authority. What they love, though, are "strategy guides"—those books and Web sites, written from a peer's perspective, with inside info on how to win. (In many games, it's just about impossible to win without these "cheat codes.") So, want to share hand-won knowledge? Position yourself as a fellow player who has been there and can offer some strategy tips, not as a boss.

5. *Watch the Map.*

Videogames are complex—just watch one for a while. But they're a lot more transparent than the world we know. One feature gamers count on is the overhead "meta map" that shows where they are in relation to other players, goals, obstacles, and resources. Young people from this generation function best if they know exactly where they are, what they need to win, and who's ahead of (or behind) them. They need a map, a guide, some external metrics to show how far they have to go and what's in their way. As you may have noticed, real life seldom provides all that. But you may be able to teach them how to develop their own meta maps—or at least learn how to operate without one.

6. *Can't See It? Ignore It.*

For gamers, the action—and there's plenty of that—is all on the surface. In a game, there are almost never truly unseen enemies. That's quite a contrast to human organizations, whether families, companies, or communities, where you may be weakened or frustrated by decisions from people you can't confront. This generation can become confused, baffled, even furious when thwarted by unseen forces in organizations. Of course, you can't make your gamer's world transparent. But you can make some processes clearer, and head off some nasty surprises.

7. *Demand the Right Team.*

In gaming, there's nothing more frustrating than playing with someone who doesn't "get it." That's why multiplayer games offer certain regions where newbies practice their skills before they foist themselves on others, and why designers create mechanisms for people who just shouldn't be in a high-level area to go a less competitive island, world, or other area of the game. Good gamers will flee places where there aren't enough high-quality players. They do the same in other parts of life as well. Groups thrown together by luck, tradition, or a desire for "balance" just don't work for them. Help the gamers you care about find teams that match their level—and their passion for a particular challenge—and you'll be amazed at what they can do.

THE KIDS ARE ALRIGHT

Planet of the Rotting Minds?

HOW VIDEO GAMES FORGED THE NEXT BABY BOOM

The children now love luxury; they have bad manners, contempt for authority; they allow disrespect for elders and love chatter in place of exercise. Children now are tyrants. . . . —Socrates

If that widely reproduced quote is to be believed, tension between the generations is perennial. The dominant group worries about the rising cohort, sometimes even condemns it. Meanwhile, the new group not only overlooks the experience of the past, but often dismisses it as irrelevant. So for people interested in practical results, the question isn't whether a new generation is coming along; that is always true. The real question is: Does the behavior of this new group change the world in any way that really matters?

If you're in business today, the answer is clearly yes. *This* new generation is huge: 90 million people in the United States alone.[1] Already, there are more of them around now than there are baby boomers (individuals currently aged 40 to 58).[2]

1

Most, about 56 million, are old enough to be real employees, real managers, even in some cases real executives. (This generation moves fast; the Department of Labor estimates that 12 percent are already managers in the current workforce. No wonder that 43 percent of U.S. employees say their managers are "noticeably younger" than they are.) So, like the boomers, these people are so numerous that, by pure volume, they are worth business attention. If such a large group is different from established norms in important ways, they almost automatically change popular culture. Where there are conflicts, they tend to win. They may outnumber their elders, and, biologically, they'll outlast them. Eventually, by reaching vital positions, they can reshape a huge part of the business landscape.

And what our research shows is that this new generation is indeed different from the boomers—very different—in ways that matter throughout business. They have systematically different ways of working. They choose systematically different skills to learn, and different ways to learn them. They desire systematically different goals in life. The way that members of this generation think about their careers, their companies, and their coworkers is a long way from what boomers have come to expect. How hard this huge new cohort works, how they try to compete, how they fit into teams, how they take risks—all are different in statistically verifiable ways. And those differences are driven by one central factor: *growing up with video games.*

America's New Favorite Pastime?

If that statement sounds unlikely, you (like many of us) might have overlooked just what a force video games have become since we were adolescents. Perhaps the simplest way to measure the power of gaming is to look at the pure size of the market. To those of us still unconsciously living in the Atari era, it is a surprisingly grown-up industry, and a stunningly large business. Games are not a niche any more. Take a look at those ads in the Sunday paper. Video game consoles and software, though also sold in specialty stores, are now staples of the "big-box" retailers—Best Buy, Wal-Mart, Target, Toys 'Я' Us—the places that practically define the mass market. Penetration of games is almost certainly much broader, economically speaking, than penetration of computers and the Internet. Some 92 percent of American kids from age two to age seventeen have regular access to video games. Only 80 percent live in households with computers.[3] By definition, anyone with a computer or an Internet connection has game-playing hardware. In addition, there are hundreds of millions of dedicated game devices: consoles that hook up to your television, PCs created especially for gaming, all those Game Boys. And whereas parents may complain about the cost, compared to computers—and to computers with broadband connections at $50 per month— game devices are cheap. One of the most popular consoles, Nintendo's GameCube, lists for just $100. No wonder, then, that gaming is everywhere, including homes that can't afford much computing. No wonder that the Sony PlayStation *alone* is in 25 percent of all U.S. homes. And no wonder that Microsoft was willing to spend $750 million—that's three quarters of a *billion* dollars—just on initial marketing for its Xbox game console.[4]

Americans now spend more money on video games each year than they do on going to the movies, and more time at home playing video games than watching rented videos.[5] In

2003, global sales for the entire game sector approached $28 billion. Deutsche Bank forecasts worldwide game software revenue to grow at 13 percent yearly over the next four years. Perhaps most telling, games have begun to displace the defining boomer technology, television. As early as the fall of 2003, network executives were admitting that video games had caused a sharp drop in television viewing among the valuable young-male demographic.[6]

As a social phenomenon, gaming is far broader than we tend to assume. Already, five out of every ten Americans—about 145 million consumers and employees—play video games in one form or another. Here in the United States, some 39 percent of computer gamers are women (the percentage is lower for game console players).[7] Nearly half of all gamers play with other family members. This surprising reality is echoed in Europe and Asia. In the European Union, console and computer games reduced the market share held by traditional toys and games by nearly a third—and it took just four years. Meanwhile, the British industry is being driven by adult and sophisticated teen purchasers, not younger kids. As for Asia, a single Korean game claims 3.2 million paying subscribers, and the Chinese game market has already reached 14 million users despite hurdles of cost, censorship, and technology.[8]

Gamers are not only all around us; they are also committed, at least as measured by the money they spend. Take a look at the market for gaming. Millions of people worldwide play complex interactive fantasy games. One stalwart is Sony's *EverQuest*, with 650,000 registered players who stay online an average of twenty-two hours a week.[9] That's like having a part-time job—only instead of getting paid, it costs you money. At thirteen dollars a month, that adds up to about $101 million a year in revenues from subscription fees alone. Some 30 million people play fantasy sports games, increasingly online. Thirteen percent of those visiting online sport sites say that fantasy games are a main attraction—so attractive that ESPN now charges $29.95 per season of fantasy football or baseball. The games are such a pull that one operator, Sportsline.com, projects about $12 million in annual revenue from fantasy sports leagues alone in 2003.[10] IDC calculates that the average gamer spends over two and one-half hours each day gaming—time that once would have been spent in front of the television or at the movies.[11] As Terry Press, Dreamworks' marketing chief noted, the movie *Tomb Raider* had to list the name of the video game character, Lara Croft, instead of actress Angelina Jolie. "Their target audience has no idea who Angelina Jolie is," said Press.[12]

The market also shows us that gaming and related behaviors don't stop just because gamers become adults. Like the baby boomers, the millions of members of the game generation will have more economic impact as they grow older and continue to play and expand their collection of games. Already, you can see the signs. In Great Britain alone, adult consumption of leisure products and activities has grown by £15 billion in just four years, industry analysts note, "as adults spend more to alleviate their increasingly stressful lives."[13]

The Industry Standard

These numbers mean that video games are a standard part of our culture. And in the United States, at least, they have been for roughly two decades. That's what created the game generation. Throughout America, video games became, rather abruptly, both pervasive and invasive. When 50 percent of Americans are playing them, then, by numbers alone, video games have become the center of the new mainstream, not the geek haven so many of us might assume.[14] As Lee Uniacke, group publisher of the Ziff Davis Media Game Group, once put it: "Video gaming is much more a part of our lives and everyday entertainment choices than twenty years ago. Gamers have become a key demographic target for advertisers and vendors. Where movies and television are aimed—that's exactly where video games are."[15]

Yet to most baby boomers in business—you know, us, the people still dominating the managerial ranks—video and computer games are practically invisible. Unless we are in the industry, we simply don't think about them, or their effects. That sounds extreme, we know. Most of today's business professionals know that games exist, of course. Games may even play some part in their personal lives, whether as a distant memory from late adolescence, another chronic worry in rearing their own children, or one more option for electronic entertainment. But they still think of them as a niche.

And that belief is where the game generation—and the generation gap between gamers and boomers—comes in. Once you really look, you discover that Game Boy and PlayStation aren't just a faintly embarrassing part of the economic landscape; they are a central, defining part of growing up for many millions of people. The first massive wave of mainstream gamers, the ones who as ten-year-olds made Nintendo so popular, are in their twenties and early thirties now. For these people, the gaming world was never a niche; they have been so surrounded by it that they think games are just another part of the real world. Members of the game generation themselves recognize that the experience defines them. Our

---

BOX I-1: WHAT IS A "VIDEO GAME"?

The world of video games is not only huge, it's diverse. There are arcade games: coin-operated machines, normally one game per machine. There are computer games, which run on (of course) personal computers. There are handheld games, either dedicated (such as those little bass-fishing devices) or capable of playing many different games (such as Nintendo's Game Boy). And there are digital games, such as Sony's PlayStation, which run on consoles and display on your TV. These differences not only include delivery platform, but extend, somewhat, into the nature of the games played there and the way users play them. But if what you care about is impact on business, all these differences can be safely ignored. Many, many game titles are available on more than one type of platform. More important, the lessons that games teach have much more to do with the basic nature of playing any video game than with the specific platform, genre, or title. *Pokemon* on the Game Boy is far different from *EverQuest* on a networked PC, but they are much more like each other than they are like any experience outside the game world. To avoid repetition (computer, handheld, or console, etc., games), we use several terms describing video games interchangeably.

---

interviewees say things like: "Unless you're living in a cave, everyone has played a video game. It's part of our culture."

And they are right. If you are a business professional over thirty-four, the chances are very good (two to one) that you had little or no video game experience as a teenager. For professionals under thirty-four, the proportions are not only reversed, they are also *doubled*; our survey shows that chances are four to one that people in this age group have had substantial game experience growing up. And, as you might know, the games they grew up on were much more powerful than those available to older groups. For them, for their entire generation, video games have been a defining part of their reality. What do we mean by "defining"?

- *Everywhere.* For anyone whose attitudes formed before the mid-1980s, video games were a fad. Huge, but a fad. For today's young adults, and the many millions coming along behind them, games are much more than any fad. For one thing, they're far more pervasive. Atari became one of the most successful technology introductions in U.S. history by selling about 3 million consoles a year; twenty years later, Sega's Dreamcast was a failure, withdrawn from the market, for selling about that many. Today's game market is huge because *nearly every kid is involved.* When the *Pokemon Gold* and *Silver* cartridges came out for Game Boy Color, they sold 6 million copies in just three months. Nintendo was able to count on selling 24 million Game Boy Advance units— nearly as many as all the Atari machines ever sold—in a single year. *Final Fantasy*, a video game series far more esoteric than *Pokemon*, has sold more than 30 million copies worldwide. At last count, Nintendo had sold 110 million Game Boy machines, enough to literally cover every square inch of Massachusetts, Connecticut, and Rhode Island. With numbers like that, whether kids own game machines or not, they have experienced them.

- *Established.* People now in their twenties and early thirties have never known a time without digital games. They grew up in a world where *of course* PlayStation was the biggest success in Sony's fifty-year history and the source of nearly half Sony's profits, and where *of course* Nintendo sold 1.4 billion video games. It is largely because this generation takes games for granted, as something found in every home, that Deutsche Bank can seriously predict that 70 percent of U.S. households will own a next-generation game console. Market penetration like that might not be quite in TV's ballpark, but it's certainly in the same league.

- *Emotional.* "I have all these warm memories of playing over at friends at 3 a.m. when I was younger with a little TV hidden in the bed . . . [and] of the first time we found the ice beam in *Metroid*," said gamer Chelly Green of some of his favorite childhood experiences.[16] And the power of those growing-up experiences doesn't fade just because gamers become adult customers, employees, and managers. As another member of the generation wrote, "Forget football and women—if you really want to bond with a man in his mid-twenties, simply mention Manic Miner. . . . memories from 1987: sitting around a small TV hooked up to a computer with the processing power of an abacus waiting for half an hour to load a game made up of about eight colors and a single moving dot." Veteran game retailers, who make their living understanding this connection, expect these same people, all grown up, to purchase millions of next-generation game machines for themselves and their children.

- **Expected.** In our interviews, we consistently find that business professionals from their early twenties to mid-thirties believe that almost all business colleagues their age have played video games more than casually. The modal estimate is 90 percent; the lowest estimate we've ever heard is 60 percent. And they're right; our own survey found that, of the business population age thirty-four or younger, fully 81 percent have been either frequent or moderate gamers. So a thirty-four-year-old manager for a *Fortune* 100 company wasn't exaggerating when he told us, "It would be hard to come across somebody of my generation who hasn't played Nintendo or Atari. They are all pretty easy to figure out. My parents' generation might have trouble. . . ." Even presumed bookworms play video games. Asked what he would do with the $12,000 prize he won in the 2003 Scripps Howard National Spelling Bee, thirteen-year-old Sai Gunturi reportedly said, "I'm going to buy a lot of video games. Like, a lot."[17] A junior manager from a multinational company summed it up: "[T]he people who play now are professionals and business people—a cross section, just normal people on the upper end of the pay scale."

Looking closely at this group's connection to games tells us (and our data confirms) that video games are central to understanding the generation. The relationship between the gamers and their technology is powerful (see box I-2), more powerful than the boomers' once-frightening rock and roll revolution, or the insidious teachings of television. And like popular music, games are a mix of entertainment content and technological delivery medium that

- was created specifically for them, as children and adolescents
- excites powerful emotions, even though it isn't a real-life experience
- is impenetrable to their parents and older colleagues
- has been literally under their control from the very beginning
- has always served as an escape route, a technology that lets them transport themselves away from the boring and restrictive world inhabited by their parents and other authority figures, and to a place that those older people—who wouldn't "get it" anyway—simply cannot follow

BOX I-2: DEFINITELY NOT IN KANSAS ANYMORE

Games are a technology that has been universally adopted by a large, young cohort and ignored by their elders. That's powerful enough to start with. But when you look at the experience that technology delivers—the content and the nature of the gamers' world—things really get interesting. Universally, and almost subliminally, games deliver a "reality" where the rules are quite different from any found out here in the rest of the world. Take a look at this quick overview of the lessons games teach:

The Individual's Role

- *You're the star.* You are the center of attention of every game, unlike, say, Little League, where most kids will *never* be the star.

- *You're the boss.* The world is very responsive to you. You can choose things about reality, or switch to different experiences, in a way that is literally impossible in real life.

- *You're the customer, and the customer is always right.* Like shopping, the whole experience is designed for your satisfaction and entertainment; the opponents are tough, but never *too* tough.

- *You're an expert.* You have the experience of getting really, really good—especially compared to others who actually see you perform—early and often.

- *You're a tough guy.* You can experience all sorts of crashes, suffering, and death—and it doesn't hurt.

How the World Works

- *There's always an answer.* You might be frustrated for a while, you might even never find it, but you know it's there.

- *Everything is possible.* You see yourself or other players consistently do amazing things: defeat hundreds of bad guys singlehandedly, say, or beat the best N.B.A. team ever.

- *The world is a logical, human-friendly place.* Games are basically fair. Events may be random but not inexplicable, and there is not much mystery.

- *Trial-and-error is almost always the best plan.* It's the only way to advance in most games, even if you ultimately break down and buy a strategy guide or copy others on the really hard parts.

- *Things are (unrealistically) simple.* Games are driven by models. Even complex models are a lot simpler than reality. *You can figure a game out, completely.* Try that with real life.

How People Relate

- *It's all about competition.* You're always competing; even if you collaborate with other human players, you are competing against some character or score.

- *Relationships are structured.* To make the game work, there are only a few pigeonholes people (real or virtual) can fit into, such as competitor/ally and boss/subordinate.

- *We are all alone.* The gaming experience is basically solitary, even if played in groups. And you don't experience all of the activity, for any sustained time, as part of a group.

- *Young people rule.* Young people dominate gaming. Paying your dues takes a short time, youth actually helps, and there is no attention paid to elders.

- *People are simple.* Most in games are cartoon characters. Their skills may be complex, multidimensional, and user-configurable, but their personality types and behaviors are simple. There's big and strong, wild and crazy, beautiful and sexy, and a few other caricatures. That's it.

What You Should Do

- *Rebel.* Edginess and attitude are dominant elements of the culture.

- *Be a hero.* You always get the star's role; that is the only way to succeed or get satisfaction.

- *Bond with people who share your game experience, not your national or cultural background.* It's a very global world, in design, consumption, and characters, and in the phenomenon of the game generation.

- *Make your own way in the world.* Leaders are irrelevant and often evil; ignore them.

- *Tune out and have fun.* The whole experience of gaming is escapist. When reality is boring, you hop into game world. When a game gets boring, you switch to one that isn't.

Not exactly like "real life," is it? And remember, this other-worldly experience has been exclusive to gamers.

So this game generation has, in an important way, grown up in a different reality than the rest of us. They have spent billions of dollars, and billions of *hours,* in the virtual worlds created by these machines. And this is a powerful information technology, unique in history, far more different from television, for instance, than television was from radio and film, the media that came just before. There is a similarity, though: Games, like television, are a universally shared, technology-powered experience. Wouldn't we expect such an experience, so deep a part of growing up and yet so different from any reality that has come before it, to change the generation that grew up with it—especially if their elders didn't take part at all? Bathing in a powerful interactive media technology, for hundreds and even thousands of hours each, during their most formative years—how could that *not* have an effect? It's enough to change what young people want, what they will put up with, and where they will go. It will make them different as workers, as managers, executives, and investors. In fact, it has already begun to change the world.

Parents see this widening chasm all the time. As one mother put it:

> I feel like I'm missing out on something now by not having played video games. I wish I knew how to play those things kids have down in the basement. It is daunting when children are playing the games with their fingers flying all over the place—it's intimidating that my children have skills that I don't have.

Gamers have these new skills because they've spent endless amounts of time honing their craft in a world that was created solely for them. In this common space, they grew up together, started speaking a new and unique language only they could understand. The only question was whether these experiences would make any difference later in life. According to our research, it appears as if that will be the case—and with more positive effect than almost any of us would have ever imagined.

More Than a Boom

Even if the game generation *is* different—will that matter to the rest of us? Absolutely. This generation counts because it's too big not to. The primitive truth is: (cohort) size matters. Careers have been made on the baby boom only because it is so large. Even today, according to the National Institute for Health Care Management, the boomers are at it again, this time driving dramatic growth in prescription spending.[18] Now the gamers' boom includes some of the largest birth cohorts, as a percentage and in absolute numbers, that the U.S. economy has ever seen—and a set of cohorts, linked not only by size but also by cultural factors, that spreads across eighteen years. Looking at the population curves, the baby boom was a demographic wave that was tall and wide, and it ramped up quickly. Each of those factors increased the generation's impact—made it a generation worth the name, in fact. We suspect that other generations—no matter how genuine in cultural or demographic or historical terms— have proven less useful to business decisions because they didn't measure up in at least one of these dimensions. Perhaps they weren't large enough. Perhaps they weren't sustained over enough time. Perhaps they arose too gradually. It's tough to build a career, or a company, on the strength of a few birth years. For most businesses, that doesn't provide enough time for a learning curve; and a generation that is only a few years wide can only be, at most, a small percentage of the total population. (The baby boom, in contrast, has typically represented more than 30 percent of the U.S. populace.) See figure I-1.

All these factors explain exactly why the game generation matters, and will continue to matter for years to come. While the baby boom included the largest U.S. birth cohort to date, the game generation will ultimately outdo the baby boom in size, in scope, and presumably in influence. The best current projections show a continued rise of annual births in the United States well into the

FIGURE I-1

Boomer-Gamer Populace

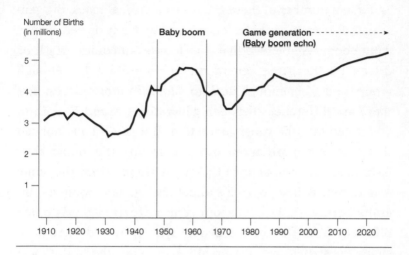

2020s. By that stage, the game generation's peak cohorts will be far larger than the peak cohorts of the baby boom. More to the point, the total size of the game generation is already far greater than the baby boom ever was. Right now, there are far more people who speak the language of games than there are boomers. According to game industry and census data, we estimate about 90 million in the game generation over the age of ten—which, as any parent knows, is definitely old enough to have learned that language like a native. Compare that to the standard census estimate of 77 million baby boomers.[19]

What About Gen X?

Even if this megagroup shares the powerful experience of video games, what defines it specifically as the *game* generation instead of, say, the "baby boom echo," or Generations X and Y, or even the PC or cell phone or MP3 generation? Three things.

First, a number of these groups lack critical mass. Big generational trends have, for decades now, been driven by the baby boom. We believe that, for decades to come, they'll be driven by the game generation. It's simply a big enough group, and a big enough deal, to matter in more places. Yes, there are differences between generations X and Y, both of which fall into the game generation. But you'll have noticed that, unless you are in one of those groups, the impact they have is small compared to the larger trends from the game generation. Believe us, we sympathize. As late boomers, literally born with the 1960s, our cohort experience was much different from that of the people who were old enough to shape the sixties, or at least really experience them. But most people don't notice—nor should they. The bottom line is that only really big groups matter.

Second, the elements that hold this group together—that help us understand their attitudes and behavior—have more to do with games than with any other element we know of. Certainly, the (rather boomer-centric, but isn't *that* typical) idea of calling a group the baby boom "echo" is long-since past and already sounds faintly silly. Millions of members of the game generation have parents born after the baby boom. As for X and Y, though these terms have gained widespread media acceptance, and though there remain some key differences between these two distinct groups, the differences are, for business purposes, anyway, rather subtle. (Stereotypical Xers are said to be known for their cynical outlook—think Kurt Cobain—whereas stereotypical Ys are supposed to be much more upbeat, like Britney Spears.) Like the distinction between early and late boomers, or like other "demos" such as women eighteen to thirty-four, Gen X and Gen Y can be useful categories for, say, marketing. For the rest of business, they just don't explain enough. You can also try identifying a very large group as the computer or technology generation, but there is a crucial difference. Younger people may take to technology more readily than their elders. But for most digital technologies, certainly for computers and the Internet, every group ends up using them. Games are different. A boomer who can't pick up a new computer program is basically just not trying. But a boomer who can feel natural playing a video game—or a member of the game generation who *can't*—is a real anomaly. The new survey data also strongly suggest that the differences created by video games bridge many of the differences between other groups. Gamers—the whole generation, including X and Y and letters to be named later—simply approach the world differently than their predecessors. Traditional concepts of value, progress, and other fundamentals of the business world are transmogrified beyond all recognition. *They* all take the new attitudes for granted; *we* simply don't "get" them. Isn't that what generations are all about?

And that's the third thing that tells us this is the *game* generation: It has produced a real generation *gap*. It's not just that boomers and gamers grew up differently; those differences have led to very different worldviews. Many of those, the ones focused on business, are the subject of our research, and are detailed in the remainder of the book. But you can see the generation gap without our survey. Simply look at the attitudes of people around you. Many game-driven changes are already visible. Yet unless they're prompted to look, boomers tend not to see them. We've already seen that games are a huge part of our culture, for instance. Anyone who actually looks at the games selling and being played knows that the typical video game is not the blood-splattering, media-grabbing, parent-stressing cartoon that makes the nightly news on a slow or tragic day. Instead, it's a massive problem-solving exercise wrapped in the veneer of an exotic adventure. Or it's the detailed simulation of an entire civilization, or a pivotal battle that affected the course of world history. Or it's a serious opportunity to try coaching a sports team or setting military strategy. In short, even if their surface is violent, sexist, or simpleminded (which is not true nearly as often as nongamers believe), games are incredibly complex computer programs that lead the brain to new combinations of cognitive tasks and demand new levels of processing power.

Once you really look, all that makes sense. Yet it surprises most boomers. *Our attitudes keep us from seeing reality.* As one industry executive argues, the video game experience has grown exponentially since the days of *Pitfall* on the Atari 2600. Games "can now deliver personality and a driven story line," says Chris Melissinos of Sun Microsystems. "The content is so compelling, it will start to outpace traditional media and draw in people who aren't playing video games now."[20] To put it more bluntly, we nongamers miss a lot because we are trapped in our own prejudices of the past. Most boomers see video games as somewhere between a major threat and a trivial waste of time. We worry about socialization, violence, sexism, and just plain stupidity. We pick up the controller and feel baffled, then bored. We wonder what those people who grow up with games are missing out on: team sports, perhaps, or reading, or even TV? When the boomers we know watch people they care about playing games, they begin to have the kind of thoughts their own parents once had about TV: "Too much time watching that screen will rot your mind." We're too sophisticated to say it that way, of course, but are fear, and prejudice, really any different?

Here, Data Data

One of the best antidotes to prejudice, of course, is real data. And we now have, for the first time, clear objective evidence to validate the experience and to show exactly how the game generation differs and how that matters to business. With the help of researchers at North Star Leadership Group, we designed and conducted a large-scale nationwide research survey specifically to ask about games and business.

Our survey included more than 2,500 Americans, mainly business professionals. That group included a wide range of ages, women as well as men, with all levels of gaming experience. It deployed a carefully selected group of questions used and found reliable in numerous past surveys—but used those items for a whole new purpose: to explore how gamers think and feel about their work, compared to nongamers. References to data from this survey are included throughout the book. Some additional results and key charts reflecting this data are included in the appendix.

This survey was different from any past survey because both the sample of respondents and the mix of questions were chosen specifically to examine business-relevant changes based on game experience. In other words, this is the first survey ever conducted to find out *whether the experience of gaming, and growing up surrounded by games, changes attitudes, expectations, and abilities related to business*. And the answer is a resounding yes. Analyzing these standard psychological measures strongly suggests that those who played games as teens are different as employees, as managers, and as executives. Some differences are already clear to any observer; others will be unfolding for as long as we boomers live.

Video games have dramatically changed the way members of this generation see the business world, how they think about work and risk and success, and what they expect of themselves. These attitudes can be confusing to boomers—to anyone who doesn't intuitively understand game culture. They can even be counterproductive, both for the organization and for gamers themselves. But the deep lessons this generation has learned in and around video games carry enormous value. If managed and reinforced correctly, they can deliver that value to individual managers, to work groups, and to entire companies.

How can managers who don't understand this generation capture that value? How can they manage and develop people who are decidedly different, often in ways that seem negative? This generation is taking the economic stage *right now*, yet few managers or senior executives—even few parents— have even noticed the things that set them apart. So how could they possibly understand the change this group is bringing about—even though it is a change we'll all have to face?

How many managers throughout the *Fortune* 500 realize that all those start-ups were fueled by the game generation, and that neither their attitudes nor their capabilities will be suppressed for long? Stereotypes notwithstanding, the data show that members of this generation have extraordinary potential to become great professionals, great team members, and great CEOs. All they—and we—have to do is understand the strengths that this odd "training program" has given them, and how to match those strengths to organizations, expectations, and people rooted in a very different world.

This book makes it possible for all of us to understand, and relate to, this important new generation. It documents the size and potential impact of the game phenomenon by looking at the generation that has adopted this technology as its own. It analyzes and presents game culture, which is obscure and even hostile to most boomers (not, of course, by accident). And it reveals, for the first time ever, how the game generation is different *specifically in ways that matter for business.* This book allows any professional to see what it's really like inside the world of video games (without burning hundreds of hours with game controller in hand). We can't teach you to play video games or even to act like a gamer; neither of us could ever pass for a native at a gaming convention. But we can take you past the surface of the game experience to reveal what the lessons really are and how they have made the game generation different. You'll get unique analytic insights into the most important generation that business has ever tried to absorb.

Got Game looks at key business changes driven by gaming. It identifies which aspects of gaming really matter to business (such as effects on management styles, risk taking, reward systems, and bottom-line performance) and which we can all leave to the generation itself (such as some of the more risqué, and quotable, elements of *Grand Theft Auto Vice City*). Perhaps most valuable, it takes managers, executives, and business professionals into the world of the generation transformed by these digital "invaders." What it reveals matters to all of us—especially if we never touch games ourselves. *Got Game* shows why computer and video games are too important to ignore—and how their business impact will be felt long after the last "game over" flashes by.

Even if you know nothing at all about video games, the chapters that follow can help any manager find out what the game generation offers, what problems it may already be posing, and how you can manage across this new generation gap (See box I-3 for our definition of "gamers."). If you know a lot about games—if you're a leading member of the generation yourself—it helps in another way: by equipping you to spot places where managers and executives from outside the game generation just don't see things the way you do, and then to translate into terms they can understand. You can even fast-forward to exactly the section most relevant to your company and your career.

As gamers know, many titles begin with brief, luscious "cut scenes"—beautiful loops assembling the very best video, music, and storytelling you'll find anywhere in the game. They're designed to introduce players to the new world, set the tone, and provide context. Even to boomers, some cut scenes feel like real works of art; they're much more like films than like games. That's why, after the first time through, most players "press start to skip," cutting right to the action. (After all, you only need to learn the context once.) If you're the impatient type, or already know a lot about playing games, you may want to do that right now. Our "cut scenes" are:

- *Chapter 1:* Space Invader: How Games Became So Important Without the Rest of Us Noticing
- *Chapter 2:* Sex, Violence, and Stereotypes: What We Worry About in Games . . . and Why We Don't Need to
- *Chapter 3:* Not the Real World: How the Experience of Gaming Differs from Just About Everything Else . . . and Why That Makes Gamers Different

Like real cut scenes, these opening chapters are important for fully understanding the world. Without this material, you

BOX I-3: WHO'S A GAMER?

The important thing for business professionals to know about games isn't whether someone plays them now, but whether he or she *grew up playing them*. So, throughout the book, when we refer to data on "nongamers," "moderate gamers," and "frequent gamers," we mean adults who report having played digital games *as teenagers* frequently, moderately, or never. Details of this theory are found in the appendix.

won't really know what games and gamers are like, unless you've had your own experience. You probably won't manage around them quite as well. But you'll still be able to take part in the action. And the action itself comes in:

- *Chapter 4:* Want 'Tude with That? How Gamers' Values and Skills Shape Their Professional Performance
- *Chapter 5:* Play Nice: After All That Time Alone, Can Gamers Be Great Team Players?
- *Chapter 6:* Win or Go Home: How Video Games Built ROI into This Generation's DNA
- *Chapter 7:* Gamers on Top: What to Expect from Gamers as Executives
- *Chapter 8:* Press Start to Continue: What's Next for Gamers—and Us?

After you finish reading this book, you'll have a firm grasp on the video game phenomenon and how it's going to affect your management team, your company, and the business world as a whole. You might even find that you're ready to play a few games yourself. Whether you find games interesting or not, you'll know why all business leaders should be able to say they've got game.

CHAPTER ONE

Space Invader

HOW GAMES BECAME SO IMPORTANT
WITHOUT THE REST OF US NOTICING

WE'VE SAID THERE IS a generation gap—a real cultural difference—between gamers and baby boomers. That gap is where a lot of new business behaviors (the ones detailed in the next several chapters) come from. But what does the gap itself look like? One of the easiest ways to see it is to visit Los Angeles in the spring. Every year, this generation gap is painfully obvious all over the L.A. Convention Center at the annual Electronic Entertainment Expo, or E3. This meeting is the game industry's version of Comdex. E3 is huge and over-amplified; it is, in precise technical terms, a zoo. There are skateboarders flying through the air. There are highly skilled, digitally hip, yet strangely shameless programmers having their pictures taken with "booth babes"—models dressed as Amazons or soldiers or medieval princesses (the only con-stant across galaxies and generations apparently being long legs and prominent cleavage). Despite the hoopla, E3 is a se-rious event. It is for the trade only: no minors allowed, no general public, tickets priced at $200 and up. People are there to do business. For many of them, the next year's profits depend on judging which titles are good enough to win shelf space, or which game consoles are going to capture their customers' attention. So there are hundreds of kiosks set up for people to try games.

But an observer who watches those kiosks carefully will notice a strange pattern: Visitors anywhere close to middle age stop to watch or to talk with developers and marketing VPs, but they rarely step up to play. The young guys—and they are usually guys—routinely go right for the controller. They even compare their scores, right there in public. Why are the responses so dramatically different? And why is the age line so sharp? It's not that a thirty-seven-year-old executive can't learn enough to try *WWE Smackdown* without embarrassing himself, or that a twenty-five-year-old can only do her job by playing the games herself. But for the former, learning would be an investment, a personal risk, maybe even a chore. For the latter, jumping in to play, even a totally new game, even in front of peers, is as natural as breathing. *That's* a generation gap.

Entertainment behavior is not the only factor that makes the game generation different. Anyone who is around them for long knows that this generation is unlike any before it. Jupiter reports that two-thirds of today's teenagers have researched or purchased items on the Internet; over one-third of preteens, as young as five, have done so as well. MediaPost Communications says one-third of teens would choose the Web as their "desert island medium"—the one piece of technology they would ask for if stuck on a desert island, more than TV or telephone. The Yankee Group says that 68 percent of American teenagers own some sort of wireless device—

that's greater than the adult ownership rate.[1] For as long as this generation can remember, technology—and the business woven around it—has been central to their lives. That is a generation gap. And we're on the wrong side of it.

How did *that* happen? Generations come and go, but generation *gaps* imply that one side, at least, just doesn't get it. It's as if some people evolved, and the rest of us weren't paying attention. That's not boomer behavior, is it? No matter how old we are, we boomers are young thinkers. We get it. We're the people who refuse to accept the limits of age; who fully expect that retirement will be as active, and expensive, as working life; who feel that nothing in life is beyond us. How did we end up in this spot, with a huge realm of artistic and economic and creative energy that we not only don't understand, but often don't even notice? Strangely, it all begins with history.

Pong Begat Atari and Atari Begat . . .

Video games have a long history, relatively speaking, and a tangled and contentious one by any standard. For the enthusiastic, the nostalgic, and the scholarly, there are dissertations' worth of materials left to be mined.[2] For a working knowledge of video game prehistory, though, you don't have to hit the library; just consult a convenient baby boomer. With some prompting, you'll get memories of the earliest games—and discover that those memories couldn't possibly equip you to understand the generation now coming into the workforce. For most boomers, their first exposure to video games in a technical sense took the form of *Pong:* a black-and-white diagram of two moving lines on the television screen, bouncing a square "ball" back and forth. But vivid as those memories are, these were not big events for most boomers (although your authors never owned *Pong* machines, they were known to obsess over them in the game's early days). By the time video game technology really matured, most boomers had found much more interesting ways to spend their leisure time—all those things that made the 1960s and 1970s (in)famous. Even if boomers had taken *Pong* and its contemporaries fully to heart, it wouldn't really help with the current generation gap; there is no real resemblance between this machine, a boomer's formative video game memory, and the video games released over the past twenty-five years.

That's why we call these boomer experiences, in all seriousness, video game prehistory. The world the game generation grew up in didn't really come together until years later. For that world, the big bang—the one event that you have to know about to understand video games and why they are so underrated in business—was the rise and fall of Atari. Millions in the game generation never experienced the Atari game console itself; they grew up mainly on Nintendo, PlayStation, PCs, and the Game Boy. But Atari started their era. It also created the stereotypes that still keep baby boomers from understanding the game generation even though *they* now outnumber *us*.

Atari transformed the landscape by giving games a beachhead in the home for the very first time. Some 20 million consoles were sold in the initial run, and 1,500 games were available. Sales topped $3 billion at their early peak in 1981, only to crash two years later to just $100 million—the price of overexposure.[3] But while the video game business nearly disappeared, video games had made it onto the cultural map. The games were still primitive and the choices few, so only a small group of people played all that much for all that long.

Gamer stereotypes may be leaping to mind about now; early gamers were often depicted as nerdy and awkward, like the arrogant loner who runs the Android's Dungeon, the game and comic shop on *The Simpsons*. That image absolutely does not represent the game generation today. But true or not, as a cultural stereotype, it has proven incredibly powerful. Driven by that early stereotype, boomer attitudes about computer games gelled, then hardened into "truths" so obvious (to non-gamers) that no one even says them out loud any more: Games are and always will be lightly addictive, sometimes entertaining, but also narrow, violent, and ultimately boring—not worth a lot of time or thought unless you've got no alternative. The fad passed, profits disappeared, and adult attention moved on. Games became a backwater.

A backwater, perhaps, but they did not remain stagnant forever. By 1988, when even the youngest baby boomer, at twenty-four, was far too old to start gaming, games were clearly back. Nintendo, which had tried and failed to reach a deal with Atari back in the previous era, tried again with its Nintendo Entertainment System (NES). It wasn't easy. Focus groups hated the clunky, new machine that looked different than anything before. But after much persistence, Nintendo created a buzz on Wall Street by touting the 90 percent market share it already had with the same product in Japan. Retailers bought into the hype, and customers rewarded their decision. Soon, NES was the best-selling toy in North America. Two years later, Nintendo's *Super Mario Brothers 3* became the best-selling video game of all time, grossing a half-billion dollars. Researchers found that, for kids, Mario was literally as famous as Mickey.[4]

The popularity of games was market reality. But adult perception was different, still stranded in that backwater. By now, we were the adults. Why should we pay attention to video games? We'd been there, we'd played them, and except for a few unusual cases, we'd quickly moved beyond them. We knew that video games were a niche market. Kids cared about Nintendo, but most adults, and certainly most business professionals outside the game industry, scarcely noticed. Thus back when today's youngest professionals were growing up, digital games passed the demographic tipping point unnoticed by most baby boomers. Only the young, gamers themselves, were truly paying attention. And they, of course, had nothing to compare this new world to. For typical American adults, computer and video games were just kid stuff. For typical American *kids*, those same games were automatically part of life—even if they didn't own one personally or play all that often.

Now You're Playing with Power

All those kids were playing with one of the most powerful information technologies ever. Not every new information technology changes the world. But a great many have done so, including the printing press, the telegraph, the telephone, the computer, and the Internet. Why would we expect video games to be any different? Like the others, they are an information tool. We know from cases as ancient as the adoption of the first alphabets that information tools demonstrably change the way people think and behave. The media we use, the tools we think with, the compressed experiences that we consume for edification or entertainment all change us forever. Otherwise, why do we place such a premium on education?

Even as information technologies go, video games are very powerful. Today's sub-$100 game consoles are, after all, powerful computers designed to run a single class of application. In fact, the National Center for Supercomputing Applications at the University of Illinois at Urbana-Champaign (the birthplace of Mosaic, the Web browser that started the Internet revolution) has actually built a supercomputer from seventy Sony PlayStation 2s.[5] The technological and cognitive power of games, as well as their content, have also grown far beyond the average professional's experience. Unless you physically play computer games with your children, you will probably be shocked not just by the technology, but by the breadth of the games being played and how consuming they can be. This power is used, as a quick trial with an experienced guide will tell you, to produce experiences that are ever more compelling. The media richness demanded by gamers and game developers drives progress in graphics and audio for the entire PC industry. The games' complex, nearly cinematic images and multilayered sound tracks give players the feeling of total immersion. After all, the game responds almost instantly to any action the player imagines, and other players (whether live or computer-generated) respond to them in real time. Even the environment shapes itself to match the players' skill levels.

The game generation grew up in this world of immersion and instant response. Growing up, a member of the game generation might easily have spent as many hours in the grip of this technology as her mother spent watching television years before. Naturally, this exposure has an effect. What gamers learned, among other things, was how to manipulate electronic information.

Of course, gamers are consumers, too; they learned that from their parents. If TV taught the baby boomers anything over the years, it was how to be sophisticated consumers of electronic information. Just look at the difference in story-telling conventions between a TV show created for young baby boomers and their parents (say, *Bonanza*, with 430 episodes during its run from 1959 to 1972) and one created *by* baby boomers for themselves and their children (*The Simpsons*, at 300-plus episodes and counting from its 1989 inception). Today's plots unfold much faster, because the creators know they can count on every viewer, even children, to know or intuit things that shows from the 1960s laboriously spelled out. Sarcasm, irony, and self-referential jokes were all introduced in television shows as viewers became more sophisticated. The boomers gradually learned to accept them; their children, the members of the game generation, take them for granted. Gamers were born knowing how to consume electronic stories. What was new for them, and unknown to their parents, was *manipulating* the stories. Members of the game generation remember learning how to make Mario sprout wings and fly. And that experience, replayed hundreds of times with minor variations by themselves and by their friends, changed them. It led them to internalize—at a powerful, subconscious level—a set of beliefs about how the world works and how they should act. Those beliefs carry over to real life. They change the way people think, the way they work with each other, what they want, what kind of service they expect, what they believe they can do, and what they are willing to tolerate. It changes the human beings inside the economists' equations in ways that matter to every business. Many studies focus on particular skills that, in isolation, can sound obscure, but that add up to real changes in our brains. As early as the mid-1980s, UCLA professor Patricia Greenfield and her colleagues established that as a result of video game play, members of the game generation show improved cognitive skills in such areas as visualization and mental maps—fairly handy skills for any professional in the age of the computer.[6] Other research has found that playing video games improved visual memory in children as young as four.[7] William Winn, head of the Learning Center at the University of Washington's Human Interface Technology Laboratory, has said that kids who grow up gaming think differently from the rest of us and will grow into adults who can process information in new ways: "They leap around. It's as though their cognitive structures were parallel, not sequential."[8] Isn't that what we would expect? Wouldn't the real surprise be finding that games *don't* have a major impact?

That impact is amplified by the way that technology and demographics combine. Yes, digital games are powerful. But what gives these games their power to transform practical life is that they have been adopted wholesale by people of one age group and largely ignored by everyone older than that. Because the younger group is unusually large and just coming to power in business terms, the technology of games will have far more impact than it otherwise might—than it would if games were following the same adoption pattern as, say, digital photography or mobile telephones. Games are simply different. That statement is true on many levels, but the most basic difference depends on two obvious and yet often overlooked facts.

First, few other technologies, impressive and powerful as they are, have ever become as taken for granted within an age group as games. Even effective access to personal computers, though approaching universal, is more restricted than access to games. Skeptical? Think of the young people you know. How many times per week do they have the opportunity to play a digital game on some sort of electronic device, whether a PC, console, handheld, or cell phone? Technology ownership of some sort is becoming universal in this age cohort in most of the developed world. As we said, one survey found 92 percent of children ages two to seventeen in the United States have regular access to video games, and 80 percent of U.S. households with children have a computer.[9] Think about it: When did you own your first computer or cell phone? Access to even one of these technology devices means access to games. And games, unlike computer and Internet usage, are not limited to the socioeconomic elite. Whereas computer access is becoming more widespread, it is still stratified by income: A household that makes more than $50,000 per year is nearly three times as likely to own at least a computer, and more than four times as likely to have Internet access, as a household making $20,000 or less.[10]

Second, few other technologies have been ignored so thoroughly by older age groups. According to the industry itself, only 25 percent of people older than thirty-four are familiar with the language of games, whereas at least 75 percent of those younger than thirty-five are.[11] And if we look at truly young ages, such as five through seventeen, there's that 92 percent figure again.[12] Perhaps there is broader or more rapid uptake among younger users. But common information technologies, the ones adopted widely enough to matter at all, generally capture and retain users from adolescence through retirement age. Even instant messaging, seemingly a natural fit for youth, is used by other groups as well. And like MP3s, another technology identified with the young, messaging is far from becoming universal. As for the technologies that are

more famously universal—telephones, television, VCRs—
these have been adopted by whole families, not by one age
group alone. Games, on the other hand, have attracted mainly
the young.

That's how we ended up with a generation gap. Reality
changed much faster than our attitudes. With the rapid adoption of the NES, digital games went from something that hob-
byists and oddballs spend time on to something every young
person plays or at least knows, from a lonely teen obsession
to a standard gift at elementary school birthday parties, from
a grade-lowering "addiction" to an automatic bonding experience for fraternity boys collectively trying out their new-
found independence and constructing their new, nearly adult
selves. The arcade was transformed from a ubiquitous teen
hangout to a much less widespread, but much more expensive, place where adults go for an evening of entertainment
often on the company's tab. We didn't notice the change in
games, or even their resurgence, because we weren't in the
right age group. Our thinking wasn't reshaped individually
because we weren't the ones playing them. No wonder we
don't get it.

All that becomes important now because, as the game generation grows older, their way of thinking will soon pass the
business tipping point. Eventually, we nongamers will have
to understand the gamers, at least a little. That means letting
go of our prejudices. Our memories might represent accurate
and even powerful images of the past—like *Pong*. But whatever
reality those images conveyed has been gone for decades,
and continuing to assume that nothing has really changed in
the video game world is both unfair and unwise. It is unfair
because the 90 million Americans who grew up playing
games do actually know some things we don't that are worth

knowing. It is unwise because gamers, who intuitively understand each other, will soon outnumber the rest of us.

Like other generational changes, this one will take a lot of established players by surprise. First they won't notice at all. Then they'll misunderstand it. Finally, the change will be everywhere at once. The world will seem to shift under their feet. That process is already taking place. The usual suspects sense that *something* is going on. Yet outside the new generation, few people notice the changes; the signals just aren't what they expect. As Doug Lowenstein, president of the Entertainment Software Alliance, says, the game industry "will never have the celebrity status that the record industry or the film industry have. People who make games don't do concert tours. They don't go on talk shows. They don't wear slinky dresses. Our creative community is never going to have that kind of visibility and star power in a mass-market sense that you're going to get from these other industries."[13] No one from the game industry has ever become president of the United States or governor of California (though many of Arnold Schwarzenegger's movies have since been turned into video games).

From a very different perspective, that of the MIT Center of Media and Culture (now the Comparative Media Studies program), Henry Jenkins agrees:

> Imagine if we were twenty-five years into the development of the American cinema, and the only thing the mainstream media said about film was that it was sometimes overly violent. We would have said they missed out on some of the major stories of the twentieth century. In a few years, we will look back at the media neglect of games with the same shock and wonderment.[14]

Could Lara Croft be elected president in thirty years?

Game Loading

Of course, this is a book about business, not culture. Do games really matter to the companies we own and manage and ultimately depend on? Have they already made a difference? Judge for yourself. Let us tell you a story.

In the last half of the last decade of the twentieth century, during the longest peacetime boom in U.S. history, the world changed forever. The change started in business. It seemed positive at first, an interesting sideshow ("Step right up, folks! See the 'new economy'!"). But it soon became clear that this change was bigger and potentially more transformative than anyone had imagined. In another peaceful and prosperous decade, fifty years before, the scale of change alone would have raised warning flags. Back then, stability was a good thing. But this time no one sounded the alarm. Not even xenophobes questioned the origin of this change. It seemed so benign, so American, that no one wondered where it was coming from. Instead, we embraced the first visible wave of this transformation from old economy to new. Pervasive and dramatic change that would have inspired horror films back in the 1950s became not something to resist, but the object of mass enthusiasm. Even now, with the changes cemented in place and the enthusiasm forgotten, most of us still don't realize how much our lives have been changed. Principles we took for granted—about life, work, risk, and reward—have been blown away. Yet most of us, most of the time, still don't even realize the world has changed.

It's not that we didn't see evidence of these changes—it was everywhere, and for a while it was almost all we talked about. Everyone, in business or out, knew that we were living in a world of new, new things. But the changes somehow

seemed innocuous. And the force driving those changes—
a force that was alien to most of us—remained deep in the
background. So we didn't question much. Instead, we reveled
in the new era. (The cover of *Fortune* practically screamed:
"Cool Companies"! "Extreme Investing"![15]) Even now, with
the new economy forgotten and all eyes nervously trained on
the only one that remains, we tend to forget—or deny—just
how radical the dot-com revolution was, and how quickly we
all accepted it. In the course of only a few years, a new business system took over, with a new vocabulary, a new hierarchy, new mental models (not to mention the much-discussed
new business models), and new power structures. Even those
of us who were actively in the middle of it have trouble remembering now how extreme it all was. A résumé full of one-
and two-year jobs flipped from liability to asset. Senior executives under thirty were a given, not a joke. So were exotic or
creative job titles. Hot companies weren't supposed to have
much structure, or any profits. And all this was fully embraced for several investment cycles, not just by communities with something obvious to gain, such as Silicon Valley,
but everywhere: Chicago, Helsinki, Tokyo, São Paolo, even
Wall Street. How could such radical change be embraced by
millions seemingly overnight?

Simple. In the parlance of that 1950s horror movie, America had been infiltrated. The millions who first embraced and
drove these radical changes had in essence been brain-
washed. The crazy logic of the boom was easy for them to accept—in fact, it seemed natural—because of lessons learned
from an alien invader that the rest of us overlooked.

The invader had been allowed into our homes for more
than twenty years. A generation grew up believing it was normal. They embraced it as their own. We adults knew it was

foreign, but assumed it was harmless. It even seemed helpful, looking after our kids and sometimes entertaining us. But its impact was deeper than we imagined. While we busied ourselves with jobs and sports and cooking classes, this novelty changed the way our children thought. Without telling them, or us, it taught them an entirely new set of rules—rules we adults would never have signed off on, but also never noticed. Subconsciously learning from this trusted source, our children embraced the new rules. When they grew up, they used these rules to create a new business world. That world— the new economy—turned out to be more game than reality. Of course it was. Because the alien force that reshaped this generation, and ultimately our economy, was the video game.

Simulation Biz

Think about what really happened in the dot-com boom. Here was an entire economy led by hip young visionaries (Netscape's Marc Andreessen!, Yahooligan Jerry Yang! Idealab's Bill Gross, who made his first fortune in game design!). This world—too big and broad and revolutionary to be a mere industry, it was a whole new *economy*—was built almost exclusively by peers from the game generation. Did all of them play video games as adults? Of course not. Had most of them played at some point in their lives? Absolutely. Were they always surrounded by games and gamers? Without question. And when they entered the start-up wilderness on that shared yet competitive quest for IPO treasures, what model was in their heads? How did they think about risk, reality, and winning? Were they paying their dues, climbing the ladder, joining the club—all those metaphors past generations have used for their careers? Or were they diving into the ultimate virtual reality stadium?

Almost no one made the connection at the time. It sounds extreme even now. But wasn't the dot-com phenomenon, at its core, structured exactly like a video game? Young participants could see it as a role-play: Assume the position of president, CEO, or marketing vice president of a major company before you reach your thirtieth birthday. You'd be managing budgets and head counts your father's boss could only dream of. This game was a little smaller in scale than *Age of Empires* (in which players can be Joan of Arc or Genghis Khan), but a lot higher in bandwidth. Or you could play it arcade style; dot-com life as a realistic *Lode Runner*. Skitter as fast as you can from VC to VC, grabbing money bags. When you've collected all you can on level one, move on to level two. Just don't fall into one of the traps that you've created for your competitors. And if this game starts going badly, don't waste time trying to salvage it. Instead, hit the reset button: Use your rare dot-com experience to move to an even bigger job, or start a new firm entirely.

Others treated the whole thing as a simulation. This wasn't a once-in-a-lifetime chance to climb a new rung on the corporate ladder, or a windfall of opportunity to be protected at all costs; it was a particularly realistic virtual world, the perfect place to try out the quirkiest business ideas and see what happens. Plenty more where that came from. Still others chose the perspective of a fighting game: If you keep your energy levels high through regular infusions of VC, you can fight off any attack that *Red Herring* might mount. Then all you have to do is slay the evil monsters (competitors, road shows, product launches) to pass the castle gates before the clock runs out. Of course, most players never made it past the drawbridge.

And this acclimation to failure is exactly the point. No matter what style of video game you play, not succeeding is no big deal; you can always start the game over, knowing you'll be a better player the next time around. That attitude, which certainly doesn't come from classrooms, television, or Little League (where failure has real costs and its consequences are immediately visible), was the underlying assumption of the entire phenomenon. After the Nasdaq plummet, most young dot-com veterans bailing out of the new economy didn't slink away in shame. They didn't curse themselves for hopping on the ill-fated ride. Instead, they pointed to the great experience they had in such a rarified world. "I won't be in the position of a senior vice president of a company again for twenty years probably," they said. "I learned a lot that will help me out no matter what job I go into."

There were other forces at work, not the least of which were the age-old impulses that always drive market bubbles. But why did this particular bubble take hold at this particular time? And why were even those who worked in the companies, not just investors, so willing to take risks? An entire generation bought into, *really believed in,* these principles that video games taught them:

- If you get there first, you win.
- There's a limited set of tools, and it is certain that *some* combination will work. If you choose the right combination, the game will reward you.
- Trial and error is the best strategy and the fastest way to learn.

- Elders and their received wisdom can't help; they don't understand even the basics of this new world.
- You will confront surprises and difficulties that you are not prepared for. But the sum of those risks and dangers, by definition, cannot make the quest foolish.
- Once you collect the right "objects" (business plan, prototype, customers, maybe even profits), you'll get an infusion of gold to tide you over.
- While there may be momentary setbacks, overall the trend will be up.

The most basic rule, though, was this: If you do bump into a "game over," no problem. You can always either hit reset and play again just one more time, or turn off the machine and pick up normal life where you left off. Of course, picking up again is what they're doing now—along with the rest of us, who find our economy reshaped by their alien ideas.

OK, seriously now: Do we *really* believe that the dot-com boom (and bust) can be explained by video games? No. And yes.

When we originally thought of linking the dot-com phenomenon to video games, it seemed like a provocative idea— just the thing to stimulate some interesting analytical questions. But even we weren't really convinced there would be a lasting connection.

Then we saw the survey data. That changed everything. The new results showed that there was more to this story than anyone had imagined. Consistently, on item after item, the respondents who had grown up playing games reported sharply different attitudes about the very foundations of business: risk, achievement, the value of experience, their own capabilities. In scientifically validated questions, in clear-cut things you can measure, in ways they themselves don't even notice, they really seem to believe that the world is their video game. That alone can't explain the dot-com boom and bust, but it probably was related. Without question, the game generation is already having business impact far beyond the Internet. The effects of video games in our economic lives will soon be hard to ignore. Firms that "get" games will unlock assets at every level of their workforces. Firms that don't will wonder where all their best employees went.

You, of course, can have much more interesting, and positive, things to reflect on. By focusing on gamers now, you are creating opportunities—for yourself, your company, your investments, perhaps your gamer children. While others are discovering that games matter, you'll be enjoying the huge potential this generation represents. All you have to do is understand them.

CHAPTER TWO

Sex, Violence, and Stereotypes

WHAT WE WORRY ABOUT IN GAMES . . .
AND WHY WE DON'T NEED TO

IT'S HARD TO FAULT most professionals for missing the business potential of the game generation. As we've seen, the accident of video game history, just an issue of timing, has made overlooking games seem perfectly natural; one might almost say business as usual. When we boomers do pay attention to video games, it's usually with unaccustomed anxiety. The first things that pop to mind always seem to be negative: sexism, violence, stereotypes, and isolation.

Gender Roles

As any labor economist will be quick to point out, changing gender roles can have huge economic impact. And most of us assume that the impact of video games on gender roles—so important in today's workforce—will be a disaster. It is easy to imagine some bleak scenarios. After all, games often present gender stereotypes so primitive that mainstream media at least claims to have forgotten them: men are hulking, muscle-bound members of elite tactical units (*Metal Gear Solid*), while women are chesty volleyball players (*Dead or Alive: Extreme Beach Volleyball*). In our survey, as well as in interviews with male and female college students and young professionals, we found significant differences in the way men and women play video games. In our interviews, men often reported that they thought women were much less interested in video games than they themselves were, and our survey data bore this out. Men, both older and younger, are much more likely than women to report that they played video games frequently as teenagers. But, interestingly enough, among our older respondents about the same percentage of women and men reported not playing games at all or that they were playing at a moderate level. The surprising difference really comes in respondents who are younger than thirty-four—the actual game generation. Here, even though more than 40 percent of all gamers are women, some 77 percent of women said they played few or no video games as teenagers.[1]

Are video games another of those gender-dividing activities, such as sports, that will keep the sexes from understanding each other once they come into close contact? What will gamers expect from each gender? Will all those grown-up adolescent boys want nothing more than a woman who looks like Lara Croft? Or someone as independent and competent as Lara Croft? Or will they only care about finding someone who knows all the secret codes to her game, *Tomb Raider*? Will they be able to handle the tension, failure, and messiness of a relationship? Or will they merely press reset every time the relationship hits a rocky point?

Our interviews suggest that reality is more complex—and quite a bit more positive. To begin with, males and females play computer and video games together. More than thirty years after the inception of Title IX, the educational amendment that was supposed to bring gender equality to student athletics, real-life sports are still almost completely split by gender. Even now, a major ruckus can be raised by a woman playing in a PGA tournament, as Annika Sörenstam did in 2003. Beyond elementary school soccer, there are very few teams on which girls and boys actually play together.

Video games, on the other hand, are more and more a common ground for the sexes. Brothers and sisters will sit in the same room and play video games for hours on end. The girls may play less, but they are increasingly nearby (see figure 2-1). And as we saw earlier, female participation rates are going up. As kids move into the dating years, it is not at all uncommon for many teenagers on group dates to have a video game and pizza party where everyone (boys and girls alike) takes

FIGURE 2-1

Percentage of Gamers Who Are Female

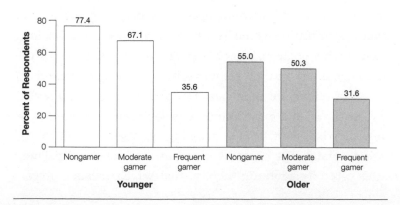

turns on the PlayStation. In college, students socialize around video game consoles—often playing video drinking games.

When we think about the way that games may change gender roles, the amount of game playing may be less important than the types of games played (see box 2-1). The men in our survey reported that when they were teenagers, they tended to like the fast-twitch games that required speedy fingers and nerves of steel. Women were more likely to favor more cerebral arcade, quiz, and puzzle games. Later in life, both genders play a lot fewer arcade games (perhaps because that category of video game is increasingly less popular), replacing them with quiz and card games. But women are still much more likely to enjoy puzzles, whereas men still favor more strategy, sports, racing, and other fast-action games.

There are also aspects of gaming that seem to go beyond sexual stereotypes—perhaps even bringing the genders together on some common ground. In a nonvirtual world, it would be rare to find teenage boys sitting around dressing and grooming a doll. Baby boomer boys could get away with such behaviors until they were about six years old. Then older male role models would intervene and tell them that it was "sissy" to be spending time dressing G.I. Joe. But in the video game world, almost every extreme sport, role-playing game, and, of course, simulation game (such as *The Sims*) includes long menus where players can choose the looks they want for the characters. Boy and girl players alike can try on thousands of different outfits, do their hair in different colors and styles, try on shoes, and experiment with facial hair. (Should it be any surprise, then, that a growing number of men in the United States can be categorized as "metrosexual"?) Then, after carefully adorning their virtual selves, teenage players (both male and female) venture out into the world of the video game and beat the pulp out of their opponents.

The interactivity of games introduces flexibility into gender roles as well. Boomer girls were socialized, in part, through hours of television. Our female colleagues often tell us that role models such as Samantha Stevens or June Cleaver often lurk somewhere in their subconscious. Boys, of course, have to deal with their inner Mannix, or maybe Captain Kirk. But the effect of games on these roles is potentially freeing in many ways. Players of either sex can experiment with gender roles in a way never before possible. Both boys and girls choose to play a vast array of female or male game characters. Even in our observation of young players—say, elementary school boys—we have heard surprisingly few negative comments about choosing to play a character of the opposite gender. It's tempting to imagine that this ability to choose a character of either gender who is just as strong, fast, smart, and likely to win as a character of the opposite gender instills in gamers the notion that anything is possible for either gender. A study at Nottingham Trent University found that 15 percent of the players in massively multiplayer online role-playing games, or MMPORPGs—a genre of games such as *EverQuest*, in which the character you choose literally represents you to many other real humans—routinely switch genders.[2]

When it comes to gender roles, games clearly haven't stopped evolving. MMPORPGs, for instance, have only been popular for a few years, compared to decades of conventional video game experience. What is clear is that the game world is not, as so many assume, exclusively male; that female participation continues to increase; and that gender-role behavior is more nuanced than nongamers tend to expect.

BOX 2-1: A STATISTICAL NOTE ABOUT GENDER

One might think that because of the gender differences in which games are chosen and how often they are played, broader findings on attitudes and work styles might be significantly different for men and women. But when we controlled for gender in our statistical analyses, the outcomes didn't change appreciably. At first even we were surprised. Then we realized that the underlying nature of gaming—not the superficial content—is what drives the experience, and thus the learning. When you look at narrow physical effects such as visual acuity, first-person shooter games have a different effect than other genres. But our data suggests that for attitudes and behaviors around business activities, the playing of games in general is much more important than the type of games played. It is the deep structure of the activity, not the distractingly provocative surface content, that has defined this generation.

Violence

In three years of research, we talked to hundreds of people about the impact of video games. One thing we know with absolute certainty: You can't talk about games, at least not with parents, and avoid the subject of violence. Parents, and sometimes the rest of us, worry that games are too violent, and that they desensitize young people to the real-world consequences of lethal, often illegal acts, which are portrayed graphically and seemingly without concern for morality.

What is behind the concern? Not nearly as much as you might imagine. There is no doubt that press reports suggest causality. Columbine-style violence is often reported in the same paragraph as statistics about the pervasiveness of game playing, such as the fact that 70 percent of kids under eighteen live in a household where there is a game console. It is also clear that there is a lot of violent content in even the most "kid-friendly" games. The Harvard Center for Risk Analysis found that of fifty-five games awarded an E rating (where E stands for "everyone," the G rating of the game industry), thirty-five contained intentional acts of violence. These violent acts ranged from 1.5 percent of total game play time in a hockey game to 91 percent of the time in an action game. Twenty-seven percent of the games showed people dying from some form of violence.[3]

Yet whereas it is easy to believe that there is a strong connection between violence and games, and a number of scientific studies on the correlation between violence and games are often cited, the results of these studies are generally inconclusive and, not surprisingly, a matter of great debate among academics. There are studies that do show a statistically significant correlation between game playing and aggressive behavior, but there are also studies that suggest that research really doesn't prove any correlation.[4] Needless to say, the jury is still out.

What's most intriguing is to look at the real-world experiences of gamers. In reality, juvenile crime statistics dropped sharply (along with crime in general) at the very beginning of the period when the level of video game violence was hitting critical mass. According to Lawrence Sherman, a criminologist at the University of Pennsylvania, "[J]ust as violent video games were pouring into American homes on the crest of the personal computer wave, juvenile violence began to plummet. Juvenile murder charges dropped by about two-thirds from 1993 to the end of the decade and show no signs of going back up. The rate of violence in schools hasn't increased, either—it just gets more media coverage. If video games are so deadly, why has their widespread use been followed by reductions in murder?"[5]

Stereotypes

Gender roles and violence aren't the only areas of worry about video games. People from outside the game generation tend to assume that playing digital games somehow interferes with normal social development. At the extreme, they worry that their new employees—or their children—will turn out to be loners addicted to escapism.

On some level, it's easy to see why. We would find it hard to deny that video games are a form of escape. They certainly look that way. The players are with us, but not really; the excitement is something only they can really feel. This tends to worry many boomers, who fear that gamers will escape into their own little worlds in perpetuity. Of course, we boomers did our fair share of tuning in, turning on, and dropping out. Yet even if our generation doesn't have the standing to condemn escapism, it does seem to have the desire. To boomers, escapism implies some mix of fear, weakness, and lack of ambition; whatever the exact proportions, this is not a cocktail we would order in public. In our interviews, this often seemed like a touchy issue—often a sign of real cultural change. Boomers worried aloud to us about escapism. Gamers, of course, have a simple reply: "So what?" In interviews, they are often at some pains to explain that of course they knew the difference between real life and real entertainment. It's easy to see why nongamers might be confused, though, since players often *describe* games as realistic; many say that games are a way to experience something they can't in real life. This notion is one of the clearest examples we have in our data to suggest that the line between reality and virtual reality for gamers is much less distinct than it is for the average boomer looking on. As boomers, no matter how often we play a flight simulator game, we would have trouble suggesting to anyone that we are doing something we can't do in real life. Thus one interpretation of this survey result can be a little frightening. Do *Madden Football* fans really believe that they are in the Oakland Coliseum playing NFL football?

Of course they don't. And this may be where the generation gap is widest. From the gamers' point of view, we boomers just don't get it. When they ask for realism, they don't mean the kind of literal fidelity we boomers might expect; they mean just like real life—but better! In other words, they mean entertainment. And entertainment is something they understand at a deep, almost subconscious level. After all, this generation has grown up in a world that honors pure entertainment above just about everything else. Gamers prefer entertainment created by sampling reality, then editing, accelerating, and amplifying it into something entirely different. To us, that's escapism: withdrawing from the real world. To them, it's just engaging in a different part of the real world—one that's a lot more fun.

Isolation

Then there's the issue of isolation—the gamer stereotype of the awkward yet obnoxious loner who is great at dealing with virtual people because he never deals with real ones. It's something many parents worry when they buy their child's first computer game. Like people watching a movie or reading a book, people involved in a video game seem lost to the outside world. Many of the games are played alone. And in a surprising twist, the most socially complex games can seem, to a judgmental boomer, the most isolating. Take the MMPORPGs, for instance. It is very tempting to equate them to a true blast from the past, Dungeons and Dragons (D&D). Like D&D, the MMPORPGs simulate human society by providing multiple players with a rigid list of quantifiable traits to choose from and complex rules to govern their interactions. Both games attract players willing to invest large amounts of time; one study has shown that players average more than twenty hours per week. That large time commitment bothers some people around online players today; we have met people one might term "*EverQuest* widows," and heard from players themselves that the game is a much more successful part of life if you can get your significant other to play, too. In fact, about one-quarter of *EverQuest* players play with their romantic partners; 70 percent of female players do so with their romantic partners versus only one-sixth of male players.[6] This heavy gender difference reflects the reality that many women play video games to forge a bond with their partners.

In its day, of course, D&D scared parents and teachers for much the same reasons video games do today. (A movie called *Mazes and Monsters,* starring a young Tom Hanks, even imagined the death of someone obsessed by playing too much of a D&D-type game, yet to our knowledge the number of deaths directly attributable to D&D remains at zero.) It is not hard to find nonplayers who assume that both types of complicated group games appeal mainly to players who just don't get real-life social interaction. If you were especially baffled by the mysterious, narrow, even vicious world of junior high school society, for instance, wouldn't even the most complicated game world seem welcoming by comparison?

All these reservations sound logical, especially for those of us older than thirty-four. But whether we share them or not, we boomers have to admit that they are essentially prejudices. However, this tough admission comes with some very good news: The isolation of gamers is one of those classic fears we can almost certainly ignore. This assurance is not an issue of perspective as much as pure experience. We can't say that video games are totally without harm. But we can observe two things. First, video games have become a standard part of our culture. If you grow up normally in this country, and in a huge part of the industrialized world, games are just part of the landscape. As most parents have experienced, that ubiquity makes forbidding video games a path of truly great resistance. But it might also make allowing them exactly the right thing to do. Growing up is largely a process of, as they say, "norming to our peers"; as Judith Harris puts it, each generation raises itself. So simply sharing the experience of your peers, even if the experience itself is without any other perceptible value, can be a good thing.

Second, it is not true that only loners play video games. They do. But so does everybody else. (Of our respondents younger than thirty-four, the vast majority—some 81 percent— reported playing video games as kids with a moderate to high frequency. Remember that from the group older than thirty-four, which includes the boomers, only about one-third reported the same level of gaming experience.) Back then, simply playing video games might have made your child a loner. Now, it will put him right there with the rest of the pack.

CHAPTER THREE

Not the Real World

HOW THE EXPERIENCE OF GAMING DIFFERS FROM JUST ABOUT EVERYTHING ELSE . . . AND WHY THAT MAKES GAMERS DIFFERENT

As WE'VE SEEN, video games ultimately grew so pervasive among and exclusive to youth that they became the defining experience for an entire generation. Since there are already more than 90 million of these people—and since our data shows that they behave differently in business—it is important to understand two things: what the game world is like, and why gamers have found it so compelling. There is an inherent message not only in what the game world is like, but in what causes gamers to have such passion for it. So it makes sense to look closely into the world of games; it is, after all, the place where this generation largely grew up. But like any cultural analysis, this scrutiny is a dangerous enterprise.

That's because, like any culture we know of—even famously homogenous communities such as, say, Japan or the Mormon church—the world that gamers come from is not just one place or time or experience. Any analysis is bound to oversimplify. Even from their earliest days, computer games have always run the gamut from simple and reactive to complex and analytical. As they have grown in power (with the relentless acceleration of hardware that we barely bother even to notice, the less visible growth in programming techniques, the artistic development that comes with ever more creators, and all the activity that a multibillion-dollar market always brings), that variety has grown more striking. But even within the gaming generation, there are schisms. Some hard-core gamers would barely acknowledge that what other, equally hard-core gamers do with their free time even counts as a real game. There are sects in the gaming community, and disagreement even within the sects. And there are, of course, countless individual variations in which games are played, how seriously they are taken, and what lessons are taken away. There are even members of the game generation who share the basic experience—including the attitudes—as a result of merely having grown up in the era of video games, even though they themselves hardly play at all. So trying to understand and talk about what the game generation is like is as rhetorically dangerous as trying to understand and talk about what Americans are like.

For an outsider who will work with this huge and important community, it is also at least as necessary—more so, really, because whereas it's hard to reach adulthood anywhere on this planet without having some exposure to American culture, the game generation's culture is, to those of us who didn't grow up in it, almost invisible. It takes place in their minds, conversations, and informal play patterns—not arenas where most adults voluntarily spend much time, or would be allowed to. Game generation members recognize and sometimes even revel in the clubbiness of their experiences. One twenty-eight-year-old manager of e-business solutions boasts that "there's a vocabulary that has emerged out of video games in the past fifteen years that only people who play the games can understand."

In this chapter, we try to get beyond the somewhat closed nature of this world. Our goal is to bridge the generation gap enough that we can all begin to understand, as we used to say, where they're coming from. Even as outsiders, we can see a number of huge differences—differences that help explain the new business attitudes and behaviors documented in the rest of this book.

Let's begin with one of the most subconscious and therefore most powerful things that gaming teaches its natives about their place in the world: They are all customers, and the customer is always right. Or, as members of the game generation might say, "It *is* all about me." The world of games is deeply, implicitly commercial. Games are a consumer product, of course. But they are also a consumer experience. Like shopping, games are experiences that partake of reality and that play on powerful emotions, but that are also carefully orchestrated to give you exactly what you have paid for. The adventure is controlled through the framework of the game itself, but universally the game puts the player in direct control of the situation, from fighter pilot to jungle explorer.

Also, similar to shopping, games become far less compelling unless the game focuses all of your audiovisual inputs on the world within the screen. That trip to Abercrombie & Fitch is much less satisfying if you are consciously aware of the eye-catching displays and the simpatico clerks. In games, the moment you stop "being" a Jedi knight battling the dark side and resume "being" an ordinary guy on the family room couch, well, let's just say that you become a little less impressed with your own light saber.

So the game world, like shopping, is a carefully constructed piece of theater. What's wrong with that? In itself, nothing. What's worth noting, though, is that many individual members of the game generation have spent thousands of hours there—hours that otherwise would have been spent in experiences that are not consumer theater.[1] What if you had spent five or ten fewer hours each week in organized sports, in unstructured play with friends, in family events that adults dragged you to? And instead spent those hours in the mall, with an unlimited budget? How distorted would your view of the world, and especially your view of your place in it, be by your own current standards?

Most of us would expect a huge difference. (And, as our data set reveals, we would be correct.) In everywhere but the game world, you have more responsibility, less freedom, and a lot less help from others to feel however it is that you want to feel at that particular moment. Unlike computer-generated characters in a video game, other people have free will. If they are parents or other authority figures, they'll boss you around. Even if they are your very best friends, they'll sometimes refuse to play what you want; they'll compete when you don't want them to; they'll suggest activities that weren't on your agenda; they'll ask for your support. They might even judge you.

We're not suggesting that anyone should trade in real friends, family, and colleagues for virtual ones, though we know those thoughts sometimes do cross one's mind. But we are saying that, unless they really did grow up shopping just about all the time, with just about no constraints, boomers and their parents have probably never experienced a world quite so superficially self-affirming as the world in which gamers have largely grown up. The pleasures of interacting with live human beings are real and indispensable. But the player's role there is a far cry from "starring" in a shopping mall or digital game. It's the difference between everyone around you saying "What about me?" instead of "The customer is always right." And the game generation has grown up, in effect, hearing the latter.

Games Are Proven Attention Getters

Another thing gamers seem to love—certainly a characteristic of their native world—is experience designed to absorb *all* of the player's attention. Games are engrossing, at times frighteningly so. Ever walk into a room full of thirteen-year-olds playing video games? It seems you could say just about anything, only to be met with a chorus of vague "uh huhs."

Why are games, even mediocre ones, so hypnotic? When something that doesn't require much attention is replaced by something that is attention-intensive, it feels like time moves faster. The game generation has grown up with thousands of opportunities to opt for attention-intensity. Believe us, it can be addictive (in the nonmedical sense). Escaping with a silly handheld game, you feel free—not because you spend any less time in some customer service line, but because you have something else to occupy your mind while you're there. ("You can control my body, United Airlines, but you can't control me!") We live in a world in which demands on our attention are skyrocketing: in volume (80 percent more feature films today than in the early 1990s! Forty thousand unique products in the average supermarket!), in pervasiveness (ads in the men's room! TVs in every restaurant!), and in urgency (more than 200 emails a day! Beeping instant messages just to say hi!). It's easy to feel, as the computer scientists say, "interrupt-driven." So the ability to reject all those interrupts, to displace them for a few minutes with something of our choice, something completely unproductive, is the best revenge.

From a cognitive point of view, it might also be something more. Part of attention management is somehow quieting the chatter, internal and external, so that we can actually think. The writer Maya Angelou tells a story of her grandmother using the phrase, "That's not even on my little mind." From that phrase, Angelou developed a belief in her own large mind and small mind. When she's working on a book, she plays solitaire so much that she wears out three or four decks of cards a month. She says solitaire keeps the small mind at bay so that she can plumb the depths of her large mind for the important ideas and profound thoughts. This may explain why one married couple of our acquaintance, both writing-thinking types by trade, goes through cycles of obsession, tiny waves of mass hysteria over extremely simple games like *Spider* or *Bejeweled* or *Atomica*. They both find that these mindless games help them to take a short break from the act of writing, mull ideas in the backs of their minds, and refocus their thoughts. Like Maya Angelou's solitaire, these games provide an escape from clutter and deadlines and complicated thought patterns, so that the mind can return to a place that is clear, brisk, invigorating—even, in the end, deeply productive.

Games Respond to You

Gamers also love games because they are exquisitely responsive to the wishes of the player. As a player in the world of digital games, you have an enormous range of choices. Beneath the surface, games constantly ask one fundamental question: What do you want to do today? Defend the earth against aliens? Search for a lost artifact? "Ah, race across Europe—very good, sir. Would you prefer a Ferrari, a Porsche, or a Lamborghini? Along which route?" You are always in charge: of whether to play at all; when to start, when to pause, when to stop; what course or scenario to experience; and what tools, competitors, and abilities to work with.

These choices matter deeply. If you've played games, you already know that from experience. If not, you can quickly learn, by watching others play, that expanding such options is one of the very few things that game designers do to reward past successes and keep players interested. (It is also the base of a microindustry in creating, finding, and disseminating "cheats" and other codes, the semisecret series of button pushes that give you even more options. Nude golf? Bulletproof heroes? It's all just an obscure command sequence away.) Games are all about choice. You have as many choices as energetic, numerous, and creative game designers can possibly imagine. Real life just can't compare.

This surrealistic responsiveness, this enormous range of options, extends far outside any individual game. If you get bored with racing that Ferrari across Europe, you can of course switch to a different course, a different car, or one of several other game modes. But you can also switch to an entirely different car racing game. (It would not be at all unusual to own more than one.) Or you can decide, "I don't want to race cars now; instead I'll race snowboards, or jet skis, or spaceships." You can stay with the same basic vehicle type, but change from racing to tricks or to combat—from *Waveracer* to *Bloodwake*. You can change genres completely, from racing to, say, fighting terrorists in the streets of Rotterdam. You can also change platforms, to a different console, or a PC-based game, or a handheld. (Here, too, it is very common to have more than one. Any ten-year-old can tell you about the differences between *Super Mario* on the Nintendo and *Super Mario* on the GameBoy Advance, and any clerk in Electronics Boutique can tell you that there are plenty of middle-class gamers, not to mention the underpaid clerks themselves, who own every major game platform; "otherwise, there's always that one great game you can't play because it's only on PlayStation or Xbox or GameCube.")

If you're a gamer, you might well be asking, "What's the big deal? So you have a lot of different choices. This *is* the modern world." But if you really look at the comparison, especially from the boomer perspective, the differences are huge. To begin with, the range of choices is far, far greater than the conventional world offers. Outside of video games, not even Bill Gates or the President of the United States can jump from Ferrari to X-wing fighter to jousting match within fifteen minutes—although that would make for a frightening reality TV series. Even more striking, in the world of games you can make any of these choices as often as you like, at just about any moment. Just try that with a round of golf or even a pickup basketball game. Outside the digital realm, games have setup time and playing time and inconveniently human teammates and opponents. You don't start a game of Monopoly or horseshoes or Hearts completely at your own whim. Or compare this responsiveness and range of options to the choices you face in activities that people chose, as children or teenagers or adults, before video games became omnipresent. Just shooting baskets in your own driveway has some constraints of time and weather and daylight. Even a solitary bike ride doesn't make sense if you have only ten minutes to spare—and once you've started, you can't stop until you reach home. Add companions and the activity's responsiveness decreases further. Make the jump to organized sports and, as modern parents know, suddenly you've got a season, defined venues, rotations, and a schedule to keep. With video games, all those constraints conveniently drop away. And the whole world seems different. How could it not?

Games Reward Technical Skills

Games reward pure technical skills that are far easier to pick up than, say, the nuances of violin playing or the ability to hit a fifteen-foot jump shot. No matter what reality is being simulated—whether it is a basketball game, a gunfight, a three-dimensional puzzle, or the creation of an entire world, from terraforming to social structure—those who have dexterity and reflexes win. The physical skills themselves are simple. The basic transaction is, after all, hitting the right sequence of buttons at the right moment. But the skills can be taken to extremely high levels. Typically, the faster you can hit that sequence, the better. In a lot of games, it's frag or be fragged. But even in the most reflective and slow-paced games, making the mechanics quick and automatic means you can think without interruption, which is more fun and probably more effective. The whole flying-fingers, quick-reaction-time phenomenon is striking. Everyone from presidents to Hollywood celebrities has noticed it. The opening conceit of *The Last Starfighter,* for instance, is that earthbound video games are in fact a screening mechanism to recruit the galaxy-saving über-pilot of the future.

Gaming is so centered on pure skill that it doesn't normally award special status even to people who have gone beyond the stage of absolute technique, no matter how triumphantly. No one, in any field, can be the young gunslinger forever. But in gaming, age and experience seem to count for nothing, except as they improve pure playing ability. Even sports, where age is merciless, offers much more: the chance to coach, communities of older players, countless halls of fame. In technology-driven careers, there are whole career paths built around adding complements to pure technical skill. It's tough to remain the fastest code monkey forever. But if you become good at project management, or keeping a team together, your power and impact and value can all rise with age. The world of digital games is typically much more stark; its motto might be "Live fast, die young, and leave a good-looking (virtual) corpse." This attitude fits nicely with the age range of those who have the time to play these games most heavily. There is a window in time when humans are mature enough to develop great technical skill—whether physical or mental—yet young enough not to let other concerns get in the way. From one side of this window, maturity looks like losing your edge; from the other, it looks like gaining the experience and vision to see that most things are more complicated than they look. And while it may in fact be wise to conclude that the simple goals of youth are harder to achieve, less in our own control, and, perhaps, less worth achieving than they looked back then, that's not a conclusion that helps get the simple things done. There is a reason, beyond physical vigor, that soldiers are predominantly young. What militaries need from the young, as much as anything, is simplicity of worldview. The young find it easier somehow to focus on a simple goal and execute it. The ambiguities of life, the real weight of the costs, even the capacity for fear, all seem to grow with age.

In gaming, too, there is no room (or need) for such ambiguity—only technique. The best fiction about gaming that we have come across, Orson Scott Card's bestseller *Ender's Game,* is built around this truth. Card imagines very young children, rigorously trained and selected, given the task of defending Earth from an alien invasion. Children are used, in part, because they can be convinced that they are simply playing a game, a training exercise. By the final battle, the prepubescent supreme commander begins to understand that his game is actually sacrificing thousands of adult soldiers by remote control (and, of course, saving the human species). Naturally, his performance begins to degrade. Extraordinary performance in a constrained environment is much easier when nothing else—nothing about the stakes or the alternatives or the uncertainties—is clouding your mind. Games have the power to increase one's ability to think strategically in a chaotic world—though we certainly hope this skill isn't used solely for military purposes.

Games Are Elegantly Simple

One thing you have to love about the world of gaming, even if you're not a gamer, is the simplicity it offers. What are games, anyway—not just digital games, but any games? They are structured, simplified, limited versions of reality. Often, the game mimics some concrete real-world activity; chess, among many others, is in some senses a simulated war. To become a game, the underlying activity must be simplified. Chess has a fixed number of pieces and a board of only sixty-four squares.

Starting from those simple foundations, enormous depth and complexity often evolve. But compared to ordinary life, there are limits. How many things are there to know about chess? How many possible actions are there? Too many to count. And yet whatever those very large numbers are, they are far smaller than the equivalent numbers for reality. War is more complex than chess. Even in a high-fidelity simulation, this gap is like the difference between the map and the terrain. No map is ever completely accurate. To be useful, it must reduce and summarize and distort reality. If it ever stopped that distortion—if it ever carried all the information that the world it depicts carries—it would no longer be a map. It would literally be the terrain. Likewise, a game without simplification is no longer a game; it is something bigger, messier, and more complex. Of course, it has other virtues: more options, more surprises, more uncertainty. It's exciting and suggestive, the kind of thing you could make a game out of, if you did some simplification.

The simplification itself is not necessarily the problem. But it undeniably does create a problem: The game world makes sense. That doesn't sound like a criticism, of course. Most of us would say that a game that didn't consistently make sense would be no fun to play. Perhaps. But it would also be much more like the world we actually live in. For anyone old enough to read this book, it will not come as a surprise that much of life, especially the parts most important to us, sometimes defies rational analysis. It's not completely incomprehensible, of course. But there are things we don't understand. Some of them we'll probably "get" someday, and others we know in our hearts will always elude us. The easy place to see that—the place we usually admit it, anyway—is in personal relationships. What do women want? Or men? Or our kids? Or ourselves? But the mysteries continue into professional life. We all know, for example, that committees take far too long, accomplish far too little, and make crazy decisions. With six-sigma reliability, they turn horses into camels. The mystery here is that we all do know that: Every single member of a committee can despise the weaknesses of committees, yet the camel gets designed anyway. Likewise, is there anyone in business who doesn't recognize the pendulum swings of a market? The local economy is booming, so everyone in town is suddenly developing class-A office space. Anyone can see the train wreck coming. The bankers, the developers, everyone has to recognize, at some point well before the crash, that demand simply can't keep up. Some of these people are going to go bankrupt. And yet, every time, the crash does come. People with brains and incentives and information are unpleasantly surprised. Sometimes it's the same people who were surprised last time.

There are technical explanations for these phenomena, some of dissertation quality, some up there in Nobel territory. But in a sense they don't matter; the foibles of committees and the swings of the real estate market will be with us forever. Even if we understand, intellectually, what it would mean to do the right thing, actually doing it eludes us. We are trapped in systems that are too large and complex for us to understand, or to influence, or to recognize our own role in.

Games are different. Back there behind the curtain, a fairly simple model is running. All the conflicts that are there at all are only there because someone designed them in, or at least designed the potential for them. Compared to the frustrating, mysterious, overwhelming world outside the screen, the universe of even the biggest game is very, very small. With only a few characters and motivations and events, and with almost all relevant information present by design, we can see logic that might have eluded us out here in everyday life. So the world of games—the world where this generation spends hour after hour, piling up what feels like experience—makes sense.

That logic, like the other dimensions that make gaming so unlike the business world, makes this experience perfect for developing skills. Training, like analysis, tends to simplify reality; it has to. We naturally construct models that reduce the complex and subtle and unquantifiable to a few things we can count and see and manipulate. Otherwise, it's too hard to work with. So young basketball players spend time playing; but the foundation is all those drills focusing on just a few basic points. Even business school cases filter out much of the complexity and noise, so students have half a chance of perceiving the central issues before the class is over. But if you've spent much of your childhood in such a simplified, sensitive world, wouldn't this one seem a bit baffling?

Gamers also love games for a simple, nefarious-sounding reason: As we have already admitted, games are an escape. Of course, the impulse to condemn gamers' frank escapism is only an instinct, and as rational beings with years of professional training, we boomers can reason our way beyond that. Logic and practical experience tell us that escapism itself is not so bad. We all engage in it, perhaps even as much as the game generation does. We can even see why it's necessary. After all, escapism in this case is just a rather ugly word for a set of activities, call them pastimes, that seem to have had a place in every culture we can think of. Games, sports, hobbies, the arts all fit into the larger category of activities that, while not strictly practical, are obviously important since they seem always to be with us, even in eras when resources are scarce, even in times that all we publicly value is work.

Listen to the things we say when we are among friends; that is, among people who share our own particular formula for escape: "This was no time for thinking. It was simply a great, joyful, moving, goosebumpy experience. I was happy. I was hearing a bunch of really wonderful songs like I never had before, courtesy of a very good hi-fi. My mood changed around. My headache went away. I went to bed happy." In this case, the writer is Art Dudley, a literate and thoughtful guy, in the course of explaining why it's not crazy to spend more on your stereo system than on your car.[2] And forget plasma screens and THX; he's emphatically not thinking about home theater, but about a record player, an amp, and a pair of speakers: a messy bunch of hardware that doesn't look like much to anyone else.[3] He's talking about having some arcane, unproductive activity transport you to another dimension, and about what that trip does for your soul. You can hear the same kind of passion, once the shields have been lowered, from enthusiasts of almost any pastime.

This ability to transport the inner person is central to the experience of gaming. And it helps make video games so important to this generation. We don't know why gamers took the lead on this one. Perhaps, being younger, they had less protection from the slow-moving lines, the voice-mail jungles, and the waiting rooms that we now use to ration such scarce resources as actual human beings' time. Whatever the reason, games have become this generation's ultimate weapon against all the dead time that life throws their way. As they see it, there is never a good reason to be bored; that's why God invented Game Boy. From the back seat of mom's minivan to those slow moments around the Thanksgiving table, you can always count on Mario—as long as some stodgy boomer doesn't forbid it.

This generation sees nothing wrong, or even odd, about packing a Game Boy for a day at Disneyland. Why would the self-described "happiest place on earth," without doubt one of the most neurologically stimulating places ever, need an additional source of entertainment "content"? Those lines, of course. The traditional experience of Disneyland is long stretches of nearly pleasant boredom (walking, standing in line, purchasing trinkets) punctuated by moments of excitement. Whatever wonders Disney's unique combination of stagecraft, characters, and machinery can produce, those punctuating moments can only last for minutes in the course of a twelve-hour day. To all previous generations, the obvious solution was to endure the waiting, and in fact to feel those rides enriched by the mounting anticipation of the waits. To the game generation, such endurance would sound quaint— or maybe just dumb. Why not choose their version of Disneyland: long runs of puzzles and adrenaline on the small screen, punctuated by the even greater excitement of similar activities that offer much less control, but much more bandwidth?

The value of this route—using games to escape from boring wait time—is not really measured in picograms of adrenaline. It's the feeling, and maybe even the reality, of freedom. It's satisfying the rebellious need to just not be in this boring spot, even though circumstances have placed you there. And we can report (with some authority) that even the brain-dead games built into certain mobile phones can provide a real emotional boost. The game we have experimented with most— think of *Pong* on steroids, played on a tiny monochrome screen using an uncooperative direction key—could never hold our attention if there were any reasonable alternative. It's hard to believe that it could hold anyone's attention. But when stuck in line, say, at the airport or the DMV, it becomes not only fascinating, but almost a registered medical device. We stop counting the people ahead of us; we stop calculating the minutes per transaction; we stop wondering whether this lunch break could perhaps be delayed *just till we've been served.* We can almost feel our blood pressure gliding back to normal.

When you think about how, exactly, games are different from what we think of as the real world, well, it's no wonder gamers have willingly spent thousands of hours immersed in this alternate reality. But can all this fun be good for them? Or for our organizations, as we hire more and more gamers? That question brings us to a little-known secret—one which, if it were ever revealed, would cause voluntary game play to drop abruptly: Games are great practice for real life. Specifically, they're a pretty good training environment for real life in organizations in which collaborative problem solving is the order of the day. Think about it. Gamers love the game world because it is absolutely unrealistic: too responsive, too focused on technique, and too simple. Aren't those the attributes you would design into a training environment? Compared to the activities that pregamers grew up with, for instance, the game generation lives in a world that is incredibly responsive. And that's not like real life, at least not like any real life we know about. Yet it is perfect for training. (Even the U.S. military—a culture that knows a few things about training—recognizes this. As far back as the 1980s, on Atari technology, the Army used a modified commercial game, *Battlezone,* for armored gunnery training. A variant of *Doom* has been used to train Marines in urban combat.[4]) After all, when we say that a system is responsive, what do we mean? Yes, it gives you options, but it also gives you feedback. The game world is a giant, accidentally created machine for giving kids an enormous number and range of choices and then immediately showing them the consequences of what they choose. True, it's not as character-building as a system that parents and teachers might design. (We've never seen a game console with a feature most parents would include, for example, the automatic message, "You said you had to have the latest *Final Fantasy*. I spent sixty-five dollars for it just last week. And now you're not even playing it!") But inside and outside the games, there is an unending stream of choices. The consequences may not seem impressive, or even real, to us: The player crashes sooner, kills fewer aliens, or loses a virtual ballgame that only she actually knew was taking place. So who cares?

The answer, of course, is that the player does. To the gamer, these consequences don't just matter; they are almost real. They are the whole point. And we can see from the time they invest in it that gaming is one of their highest priorities. So gamers make a lot of choices, in a wide range of settings, in a short period of time. And they automatically care about the outcome. If that's not a powerful training environment, what is?

The very distortions that seem most unreal about gaming have made it not just a wonderful place to grow up, but a place that created in these millions of rising professionals enormous potential for business success—if we can recognize and manage their unique generational traits. This potential is within our grasp only because the world of games, which looked like a ridiculous waste of time, turned out to be boot camp for the future of business.

CHAPTER FOUR

Want 'Tude with That?

HOW GAMERS' VALUES AND SKILLS SHAPE
THEIR PROFESSIONAL PERFORMANCE

TRADITIONALLY, WHENEVER YOU have a generation gap, it includes suspicion from the dominant group about just what the rising cohort is prepared to contribute. Think of the quote from Socrates in the introduction—don't younger people always seem, on average, a little less industrious than people your own age? We've certainly heard our share of boomers questioning the work ethic of twenty-somethings. Yet we believe that such judgments miss an important reality, and the opportunities that go with that reality. In fact, five of the values that most set this generation apart from our own have surprising potential to drive great professional performance.

Driving for Excellence

The surprise begins with the game generation's cleverly camouflaged commitment to professional excellence. Obviously, this commitment is great news, if we can really believe it. More than any time in boomer memory, business success now depends on dedicated, focused employees. The downsizing of the 1980s and early 1990s—which proved nearly irreversible even in very good times—has made sure of that. Organizations are so thin, customers are so demanding, competition is so tough, and challenges are so unpredictable that the old control mechanisms simply won't work. Fear is not enough. Greed is not enough. Linear, command-and-control systems with formal measurement and incentives are not enough. Every business needs fully engaged, internally motivated employees. You need their best efforts, their creativity, their judgment. You need their ability to go outside their comfort zones and solve problems, all the while understanding how the problem and the solution fit into the organization's ultimate goals.

Of course, managers already know this; they face the problem every day. And one lesson of the dot-com era is that it is possible to meet this challenge. Even with young and inexperienced employees, you can get the kind of focused performance the market increasingly requires. Everyone also knows, courtesy again of the dot-com bubble, that even high-performance employees can't make up for a flawed business model, or a market with ten times too many competitors, or a thousand other sins of management old and new. Smart, focused employees aren't all you need, but in this flexible and fast-moving economy, you cannot win without them. That fact brings us to the part no one knows—news that is extremely good for boomers and gamers alike: *All that experience with video games has made these people passionate about adding value.*

You have to look closely, at first, to see that passion. Initially, what you see is the value gamers put on skill. This judgment is most visible in self-assessments. In our survey, those who grew up gaming are more likely than nongamers to describe themselves as "knowledgeable." Those who were frequent gamers as teens are over 50 percent more likely to say "I am considered a deep expert in my work." It is less surprising that more than half of the thirty-four-year-old and above crowd consider themselves experts at their jobs; even in this age group, those who are gamers think more highly of their own abilities. But it is borderline astonishing that almost 50 percent of gamers—quite a young group—think of themselves as experts, with game experience driving that average up significantly. They are so confident of their skills, in fact, that they believe they don't have to work as hard as other people. Our survey showed that within this new generation, the *more* experience respondents have with digital games, the *less* likely they are to describe themselves as hard workers. (Yet, as we'll see later, they still believe that their performance will be better than average.)

Of course, upon seeing so many former frequent gamers now grown up but still as young as their early twenties—publicly award themselves the title of expert, one possible reaction is to dismiss them, and perhaps the whole group, as arrogant. Certainly, they have high self-confidence in their workplace. Their high self-regard is not just about status; in performance, in making real decisions, they explicitly believe that they are crucially more competent than the people around them. Within the game generation, two-thirds of those with high game experience, for example, agree that "If something needs to be done right, I'd better do it myself."

(This is almost—but not quite—the same response as frequent gamers in older groups, who can be seen as a kind of evolutionary link to the game generation.)

Still, no matter how deep this self-confidence is, one could argue that it's misplaced. A cynical boomer might ask, "Wouldn't you be confident, too, after a lifetime of meeting carefully modulated and dramatically enhanced challenges, as well as usually getting your own way?" On the surface, that argument is plausible. But there's another possibility, too; one we think is more likely: Gamers' confidence could be justified. A Discovery Channel documentary on the subject of the game generation might summarize it this way:

> Gamers have amassed thousands of hours of rapidly analyzing new situations, interacting with characters they don't really know, and solving problems quickly and independently. Admittedly, they have gained that experience in a simplified world focused almost entirely on themselves. But that world has also emphasized tangible results and given them constant, critical feedback. Isn't such a world in essence a well-designed training environment—especially compared to watching TV, shopping, or many other activities that digital games have probably displaced? Even compared to team sports, aren't the skills they are learning more directly relevant to professional work?

Seen from this perspective, even skeptics would have to concede that gamers might actually have learned something useful from video games, and even gained new strengths. In the end, of course, it doesn't really matter. If the game generation overestimates its talents, experience will almost certainly provide calibration. But placing a high value on competence—wanting to be an expert in the first place—that's something hard to train into people. It's a driving value that most managers are delighted to find in their employees.

A Generation of Lombardis?

From a manager's point of view, members of the game generation have a complementary value that is even stronger: their attitude toward competition. To put it mildly, gamers believe that winning matters. Even when faced with the most extreme version of that sentiment we can think of—"winning is everything"—a substantial minority of the game generation agrees. Gamers' investment in winning makes perfect sense; if much of your voluntary life has literally been a game, then winning might well seem to be just about everything. And, to gamers, digital games feel as real as any game of baseball or round of golf. As a college student told us, "When you play video games, it's a competitive thing. Having the controller in your hand makes you feel powerful. When you beat one of your friends in a game, it feels just as good as beating them in real life."

The value they place on winning extends far beyond games; the game generation sees competition everywhere. That's perfectly natural; after all, they have largely grown up in a place where just about the only way to relate to any other character, living or silicon, is through competition. So they believe, quite literally, that competition is the law of nature (see figure 4-1). It's the lens through which they see the rest of the world. As always, the lens itself becomes invisible. And, for this group, competition is most definitely the lens in

FIGURE 4-1

Competition Is the Law of Nature

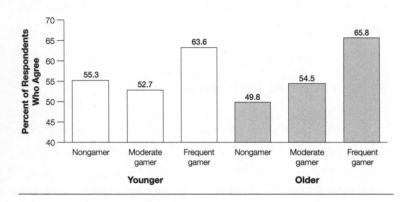

question. Compared to nongamers from the generation before, every group in the game generation is more likely to believe that competition is the law of nature. Frequent gamers, who by definition spent more time with games while growing up, are dramatically more likely to believe that.

Clearly this belief in competition gives the game generation a welcome drive to perform. Still, one might entertain nagging doubts about where that drive is focused; we did. After all, video games are not mainly about teamwork, and the goals of the game are sometimes specifically antisocial. Yet as you will see in the following chapter, the game generation has highly developed teamwork skills and a strong desire to be part of a team. Gamers are focused on their skills and on competition, but they care *more* about the organizations they work for than other groups do—not less.

Two things are striking about these results. First is the surprisingly small difference between generations (see figure 4-2). Older respondents (with an average age of forty-nine) are not dramatically (fifty-three percent) more likely to say that they

FIGURE 4-2

I Really Care About the Fate of the Organization I Work For

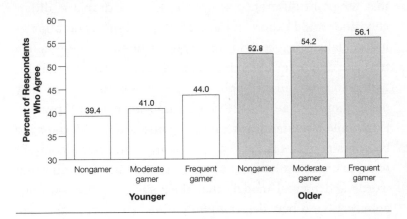

care for their organizations than gamers (forty-three percent) are. We would expect older respondents to feel much more committed to their organizations. Age, after all, tends to bring increasing tenure, and tenure means more people and experiences and outcomes to care about—assuming the match was good to begin with. In addition, age normally brings increasing rank, and the higher one rises in an organization, the more of that organization presumably becomes relevant. Less attractive, but at least equally important, age reduces our personal options; it becomes more difficult to start over, which means that we might force ourselves to feel, or at least express, some attachment to the organization that we no longer feel so free to escape from. Finally, there are the results of self-sorting. Don't we all believe, or at least want to, that as their careers go on, most people find organizations and roles where they are more happy, not less? This belief, too, would drive them to care about the organization.

Whereas it is true that the older group is more likely to say "I really care about the fate of the organization I work for," that ten-point difference is not the kind of dramatic difference one would expect. If the stereotype of this generation as individualistic, egocentric, and hypercompetitive were in fact true, we'd look for a much bigger difference. Faced with this data, then, we might begin to wonder whether those easy perceptions of gamer attitudes as arrogance are simply cultural misunderstandings. Young gamers and middle-aged boomers could both be trying to convey the same commitment to organizations and outcomes, but with such different words and mental models that their shared values—a huge potential bond between the two groups—are lost in the generation gap.

Loyal Till the End

That possibility is echoed by the second striking implication of this item: *Odds are that the more you played games as a youngster, the more you care about the company you work for.* At first glance, this statement seems to conflict with the responses we got when we asked if they would prefer to take a job with a different company in the near future; gamers are more likely to say yes than nongamers are. It's easy to assume that such respondents don't care about the companies they work for. What might be more accurate, though, is that gamers *do* care, intensely. If a highly motivated employee is frustrated by her organization, she might be more willing to consider a change. The unrecognized generation gap might also be making it difficult for gamers to find organizations that understand how to use them in a positive way. From this data, it is hard to be certain. What is clear, though, is that game experience seems to increase organizational attachment. Again, the critical point is not the size of the effect, but the direction—exactly the opposite of what we boomers might expect. Whereas the increase is not dramatic, the consistency across generations is. No matter how old you are, if you are a gamer, you probably care more about the company you work for than a nongamer. And if we factor in the way that organizational commitment would normally be expected to increase with age, it is quite likely that professionals from the game generation are more committed to the company than baby boomers were at the same age.

A final surprising twist of data provides even more clarity on the value gamers place on competition. It speaks to gamers' attachment to their firms as well as to the nature of their professional drive. Despite digital games' focus on the individual, despite the constant competition, despite the hints of Machiavellianism in some gamer attitudes, growing up with games does not seem to systematically increase individualism. The vast majority of all respondents, of all ages and all levels of game experience, agrees with the statement "I often do my own thing." In an individualistic culture that has been dominated for decades by a famously individualistic generation, this is hardly a surprise. What is surprising is that gamers don't seem consistently different on this measure from anyone else. In general, younger respondents are more likely to do their own thing, and the most frequent gamers are more likely to answer affirmatively than are other groups. But business professionals who didn't play games *at all* as teenagers are the next most likely group. Moderate gamers are the least likely to be exceptionally individualistic on this measure—and their scores are identical for both generations.

So despite the game world's relentless focus on the individual, when it comes to real-world professional attitudes, it seems that even heavy long-term exposure to games hasn't made players more rebellious, iconoclastic, or even independent. They have solved a lot of problems on their own, built a lot of skills, and developed a lot of confidence in themselves. But they are no more likely than anyone else to place themselves above the group. They want to be skilled, they want to win, and they want to be part of the team—real contributors to the team—as they do so.

Fully Engaged

Gamers have the drive to be great professionals. Do they have the commitment? One of the most striking gamer behaviors moves a number of boomers, including parents, teachers, and supervisors, to raise that question. After all, this generation seldom looks, to us, like they are concentrating on work. There's always music in their cubes, or seven windows open at once on their PCs. This generation seems convinced that it really can multitask.

Nothing in our survey addressed the issue of multitasking, but in our interviews, it proved to be a generation gap–defining issue from which we could not escape. And little wonder; this concept was, after all, the battle cry of the Internet-happy 1990s. Teenagers did it all, all at the same time: listening to music, talking, reading, trading IMs, watching TV, and—the age-old staple of teenagers—eating. All of this activity drives boomer parents—especially the fathers—crazy. The women we interviewed might believe that the younger generation could actually be multitasking. After all, women know it's possible; they've been doing it for years. Men, at least according to our interviews, consider themselves less able to multitask—and consequently they are more skeptical of the concept in general. In fact, men from the baby boom seem hard pressed to believe that multitasking is even possible. And on a technical level, there is a fair amount of evidence that they are right.

The available scientific evidence suggests that the brain seldom truly multitasks. Instead, it processes information in a linear fashion. As Hal Pashler, a professor of psychology at the University of California at San Diego, puts it, "There's less concurrent processing than you might think; the brain is more of a time-share operation."[1] If you don't count subconscious and autonomic processes, the brain mainly works one task at a time. When it is moving between tasks, the brain actually stops for a few milliseconds. So constantly moving back and forth between tasks actually slows the completion of any one of them. And the more complex the tasks, the harder it is for the brain to move between them. But we all know this from experience, don't we? When you really have to concentrate on something, you really have to concentrate.

So why *don't* gamers seem to concentrate as often or as visibly as we do? Why do they think they can multitask better than their parents? Two explanations seem likely. First, for gamers, multitasking might really mean concentrating in the face of tremendous odds. When we were kids, it was pretty easy to get away from media interference and find a place with some peace and quiet where concentration was easy. The value of quiet concentration was trained into us, and we were trained to need it. Today, many boomers still have trouble focusing if a radio or TV is blaring in the background. In contrast, many in the game generation would argue that they can concentrate in the face of all obstacles. In fact, some of them say they actually prefer to work in a noisy environment so that they can surface from deep thought to a place that is filled with visual or aural stimulation for a rest. Then they can return to the place of concentration when an idea has come to them. You don't have to look much further than your local Starbucks to find these personalities (and their laptops) in abundance.

As we know from our own experience, it is also easier to do two things at once if one of them is fairly routine. Many adults don't mind carrying on long and fairly complicated conversations while driving the car on familiar routes, but don't ask a sixteen-year-old who is just learning to drive to do the same. The prefrontal lobe needs to focus exclusively on an unaccustomed activity. As driving becomes more routine, driving activities will be loaded into deeper structures, freeing up the cortex for newer activities—like scintillating conversation. That difference in processing is why you can read the back of the cereal box while you are tying your shoes. You've probably noticed that, unlike you and your adult friends, a seven-year-old probably can't do that, even though she can tie her shoes and read the cereal box, separately, just fine.

Games might have trained a whole generation to multitask a little more easily, or to routinize tasks the rest of us have to actually think about. Certainly, they've created a taste for being immersed in data, being forced to perform rapid task switching. Not only have kids learned to concentrate on a computer game with music playing and TV blaring in the same room, but many of the games are all about fighting off one foe while three others attack you at the same time. This sensory overload was the case from the very beginning. In the earliest *Space Invaders* games, you had to keep track of the

advancing invaders, the constantly eroding barriers that protected you from their attacks, and the side-to-side motion of
your own craft on the bottom of the screen—all at once. After
a few hundred games, you could actually get pretty good at
holding all of the elements on the screen in your mind at the
same time. You were only concentrating on one activity—the
game—but within that game, there was a lot going on. (And
as the game generation would be quick to remind us, *Space
Invaders* was a very simple game.) Mastery of almost any
game is all about knowing which activities you can relegate
to back-of-mind attention, and which you have to keep in the
front. Switching from back-of-mind to front-of-mind might be
the skill set most important to gamers. Practice helps with
this skill, and it would seem to be a real asset in today's workplace. Yet the gamers' tendency to multitask can still cause
problems. Their boomer colleagues—like (we hate to say it)
their parents—might need to be convinced of this strange
ability. Even then, to those of us who grew up before multitasking was even a word, working on two things at once
might always mean not working at all.

Living in the N-Dimension

Whether or not true multitasking is possible for humans (we
won't pretend to solve that debate), the fact remains that
gamers think they do it—and they love the feeling of being
immersed in data. For a number of industries, this comes not
a moment too soon. There's technical support, of course. But
even at higher levels, these new attitudes are valuable. The
demands of business require much more complicated data
analysis tools, and a workforce that can use them.

Why? Because rapid change, relentless global competition, and exploding complexity have turned even mundane decisions into problems of genuine uncertainty. For more and more basic operational questions—what technology to build into the next product, how much to invest in a given region, whether to add that new production line—the annoyingly familiar answer is "it's anybody's guess." The more information we get, the less we seem to know about the questions that matter. Advanced decision-support technology has almost kept pace. But the average professional, even in highly competitive companies, has not. A professional workforce used to two-dimensional thinking suddenly faces an n-dimensional world. (Maybe all n dimensions were always there. But now we have the data to see them, the levers to respond, and the need to do everything we can to compete.) The tools we are comfortable with—linear models, printed spreadsheets, single-point estimates, and rules of thumb—simply can't guide us through the complex, volatile, and sometimes unknowable factors that now drive many decisions, or should.

The potential offered by a generation already used to thinking in these ways—really living in "dataspace," begging to handle more simultaneous data streams than their parents even imagined—is extremely promising. Cutting-edge analytic tools that look a lot more like video games than office suites have already helped serious decision makers produce real progress on problems that seem impossible to analyze (at least, without data that simply doesn't exist): global warming, terrorist threats, and long-term investments in infrastructure.[2] But as they continue to evolve, these tools are making two new demands. First, they require groups of managers, executives, and professionals who can become comfortable with the technology that makes these tools possible at all.

Using this technology is a purely digital, interactive experience. There *is* no hard copy to fall back on; the tools don't really produce a final report—not even a bottom line. Instead, they create impressive value by helping teams actively explore the uncertainties that make so many decisions so difficult. That exploration is an active process of really going inside the elaborate graphical displays, manipulating many different variables and assumptions, and absorbing what happens in real time. It's a shared experience, like a concert. It is, beneath the surface, a lot like playing a video game. And, as with video games, those who can rapidly become comfortable with the technology get much more out of the experience than those stuck in the simpler world.

The second demand of those emerging strategy tools flows from the first. The only real output is the *experience* of using the tool, and the new understanding that emerges from it—an understanding difficult to reduce to words or numbers that stand on their own. So this analytic experience must ultimately be more integrated into the business itself—used by the decision-making group, working together, and fed with real data. This kind of analysis can take groups to much more effective understanding and better decisions, but it's the ultimate "I guess you had to be there" experience. The boundary between analysis, decision, and action will have to become almost invisible. Working in this way obviously calls for people with new capabilities. You don't just need a few new statistical boffins or quant jocks in strategic planning; you need line managers and operating executives who can dive into the complex, imaginary data space represented by a digital graph, happily work with each other through this structured, high-tech medium, and ignore any artificial boundary between digital reality and the world "out here." In other words, if you're one of the millions who now has to manage deep uncertainty, advanced strategy tools can help, but you need some managers raised on video games. They'll not only be able to use the tools; they can probably even help nongamers use them, as well.

Driving Results

Once you see how different gamers are, in certain ways, from the professionals we are all used to, you might begin to worry. How can you manage people—how can you motivate them to begin with—if their values are so different? Some gamer values, from a boomer perspective, are really out there. The game generation's relationship with data, for example, is a bit mysterious. It's a classic generation gap issue; we see there's something there—they love multitasking, they love being immersed in data—but most of us can't imagine feeling that way ourselves. Yet in a key domain for managers—expectation of rewards for their work—the rising cohort is not just like us—they are like us, but more so. Gamers expect high rewards for the value they create. Other surveys tell us that the perceived importance of generous pay and perks normally grows with the achievements, expectations, and responsibilities of increasing age. So for such a young group to be as focused on high material rewards as our survey demonstrates that gamers are, is striking. As you read the next section reviewing gamer attitudes toward money, try to imagine the baby boomers during the anti-establishment period of their twenties clamoring for higher pay and more perks. Even more remarkable is the fact that attitudes toward salary and benefits are so highly correlated with game-playing experience.

Our survey questions revealed a shared attitude among gamers: If they do the job, they expect the rewards.

Work for the Money?

It's important to realize that the drive for recognition in the form of monetary reward is different from simple greed, or even from ambition. Look at a key measure: how the game generation feels about a strong, direct, enforced link between the value they add to the company and the value they receive from the company. As we see in figure 4-3, gamers are much more likely than nongamers to say "I prefer pay and bonuses based on actual performance rather than a set salary." This preference holds true for both older and younger populations. (The older, pregame-generation group is more likely, on average, to make this choice than younger respondents are.

FIGURE 4-3

I Prefer Pay and Bonuses Based on Actual Performance Rather Than a Set Salary

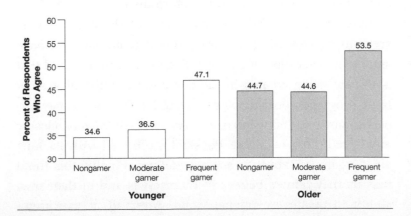

This, however, is an age- and experience-related trend we see in other populations as well. It's easy to understand; awareness of pay-for-performance options, actual experience with such arrangements, and trust in the organization to "play fair" in both measuring and paying for results are all likely to increase with age. It's remarkable, then, that the much younger game generation is so close in these attitudes to people with considerably more real-world experience.) Although the general trend is that moderate gaming experience might increase this focus on personal performance—and certainly doesn't diminish it—the real story is in the difference between frequent gamers and all others. In both populations, the individuals who have had the most extensive experience with computer and video games are the same people most likely to choose pay-for-performance.

Think about what this choice means. First, it tells us that business professionals who have also been gamers intuitively understand that their personal success depends on adding value to the enterprise. Too obvious to mention? Something every employee knows? Think about the professional behavior of people you have managed recently, or even encountered as a customer. Still sure the pay–performance connection is so obvious? Second, it tells us that many of the millions who grew up taking video games for granted are not, as some have argued, a generation of slackers. Even if you understand that aggregate value created in the company is what ultimately funds your compensation, you would only choose pay-for-performance if you wanted *your personal contribution* closely monitored. This, of course, does not mesh well with slacking off. So gamers expect to actually deliver. Finally, this trend tells us that gamers believe in themselves and in their own ability to create exceptional value. After all, if you aren't fairly sure that your performance will be not only good, but *substantially, visibly* better than average, you don't choose pay-for-performance.

Obviously, this self-confidence is a great attitude for most business settings. But there are potential problems. The least important is that, as with most surveys, these attitudes are assessed and reported by the respondents themselves. No one knows how accurately they reflect actual performance. This uncertainty may not matter, though; even if all gamers know is that they *should* be focused on creating value, that's a terrific start—the opposite of the supposed slacker creed. A slightly more important concern is that, as we saw earlier with other measures, choosing pay-for-performance implies that gamers have given serious thought to their own roles in the business world, but not necessarily much thought to the roles of others. One can imagine them being ambitious for themselves only, not for the work group or the enterprise. To be clear: There is no evidence here that gamers ignore or underestimate their colleagues' need for rewards. But there is also no evidence here to disprove that. Again, though, for many purposes the difference isn't all that important. We know gamers want to be part of a team, as you'll find out in the next chapter. We know they want to achieve results through others. So untangling the drive for personal success from the drive to create team success might not be necessary. It's always difficult. (Indeed, aren't modern incentive systems designed exactly to make that tangle even more intricate?) If high performance is the result, does the motive really matter?

The biggest danger, however, is that the game generation's passion for adding value can be so easily misconstrued. When we first started reviewing these survey results, we found the word *arrogant* coming readily to mind. The tendency of twenty-something gamers to describe themselves as experts, for example, can certainly seem that way. But when we connect their focus on skill and expertise with their desire for professional respect and their willingness to be paid only for results, we sense a very different pattern. Gamers are revealed not as spoiled kids who never grew up, but as young professionals who know that results matter, who respect the skills that produce results, and who believe in themselves. They are confident that, under the pressure of real-world performance, they will bring the commitment, the drive, and the professional skill it takes to deliver results. They are so confident, in fact, that they are willing to bet real money on it.

Latent Heroes

Taken separately, the drives we have seen so far produce an interesting pattern. Gamers are motivated by skill, competition, rewards, and the sensory excitement of swimming in dynamic data. But it's only when you combine these drives and think about the world in which gamers grew up that you really understand what the typical gamer is about. And that provides a powerful additional lever for those of us who manage gamers. It points to an inner drive built deep into the psyche of this generation: *Unlike boomers, gamers want to be heroes.* In their world, after all, heroism is what it's all about.

To see why heroism is so important to gamers, simply look at the world of games. Even scanning shelves in a good game store, it becomes obvious that an enormous amount of artistic and intellectual effort has gone into creating the world of video games. Real money has been invested, true innovators have been hired (or have somehow found a way to get their creations published), and competition for money and pride has driven major efforts. Yet the content of the games can seem a little—we hate to sound stodgy here—repetitive. Part of that redundancy is the limited range of game settings. (In movies, they would be called *genres*. But in the game world, *genre* means the type of action you, the player, get to engage in: Is it a role-playing game, a first-person shooter, a strategy title, or something else? See table 4-1 for examples of game genres.) There are all the medieval games, the science fiction titles, the military games, even the fantasy worlds that— again, to an outsider—all seem to run together. Part of that nagging repetitive feeling does come from the sameness of game industry genres. It's not true that once you've played one shooter, you've played them all. But conventions have been established, consumer expectations have been set, and individual game engines have even been reused, so the difference between one strategy game and another may not feel like much unless you are a strategy aficionado.

The bigger cause of that déjà vu, in our experience, is that the point of view never really changes. That's because the main character is always the same: you. Everyone who picks up the game controller has to shoulder the hero's burden. That's just the way the game world works. It's what the customer expects.

An artistic problem with making the player the main character is that it makes repetition almost inevitable. A moviegoer may have seen dozens of romantic comedies. He could probably even describe five or ten fairly standard character types found in comedies, and then translate all other characters into those terms: "He's Tom Hanks from *Sleepless in Seattle* with a little of Will Ferrell in *Elf*." (You can even do that, as *The Player* famously demonstrated, with entire movie

TABLE 4-1

Video Game Sales by Genre in 2002

Console Games		PC Games	
Genre	**Percent of sales**	**Genre**	**Percent of sales**
Action	27.1	Strategy	27.1
Sports	17.6	Children's	14.5
Racing	15.7	Shooter	11.5
Role-playing	8.7	Family entertainment	9.5
Fighting	6.4	Role-playing	8.7
Family entertainment	4.7	Sports	5.8
Shooter	4.6	Racing	4.4
Other	15.2	Adventure	3.9
		Simulation	3.5
		Other	11.1

Source: Electronic Software Alliance

plots.) But no matter how little variety the movies offer us, there are always more people to identify with than just our-selves. And in a movie or a novel, we don't have to be the hero at all. You can watch the Tom Hanks character almost lose his chance at love without feeling that you are losing yours; you can wish to be as likeable as Will Ferrell without pretending to wear tights and pointy shoes or building Lego masterpieces overnight.

But in the game world (with the exception of certain MMPORPGs, such as *EverQuest*), you really don't have a choice; you're either the hero, or you're not playing at all.

Glory Without Compensation

Money and power aren't usually major factors in games. But there is no doubt that the game world prizes heroism. It is not only that you play the star of the show. (Though that is important; as one gamer told us, *"Nightfire* lets you be James Bond for hours at a time, without messing around with tired story lines. Your job is to kick the mad genius's ass, not dabble with martinis and such.") It's not even that you're probably working more or less alone. In many, many games, the fundamental story is almost a generic hero's quest. The world portrayed to you in those opening moments of lush full-frame video needs to be saved. And you, of course, are the only one who can do it. Somehow your courage and skill will change history, earning you whatever simulation of fame and glory the designers can come up with—and, far more important, the knowledge, in that fleeting moment when the game is won and yet you haven't returned to the world on this side of the screen, that you are in fact a hero. (Or at the very least, you will amaze some invisible audience with your skill—a different kind of heroism.) In the Xbox title *Halo,* for instance, you become an alien-battling character called "Master Chief" who is—of course—humanity's best chance to survive. It makes sense that this model so pervades the game world; it's an easy sell. The hero's role is a perfect fit for the core customer, a young person who has outgrown actual childhood but can't yet imagine midlife crisis.

During all those hours of gaming, adolescents are like our image of the ancient Greeks or native Americans—a people who value heroism more than the things that we now assume drive everyone: power, money, perhaps even love. These are not the cultures that give rise to profit-maximizing *homo economicus*. They seem to have an appetite, at least in concept, to be heroes or die trying. (Of course one of the famous points about adolescents is that avoiding death doesn't seem to figure large in their psyches. And, death in the virtual world being somewhat fleeting, for gamers even the "die trying" part isn't so bad.) So this is the kind of world the games take place in—medieval and sci-fi and military settings and other missions that, at least in the stories we tell ourselves, cry out for a hero.

Thousands of hours in the hero's shoes may not be the most obvious preparation for what boomers call real life. One reason is that, in most work groups, there may be room for only one hero, or maybe not even one. How many companies struggle for better collaboration "across the silos"? How many organizations have been matrixed into incredible complexity specifically to help lone-wolf leaders, hyperattentive to their own bonuses, work together? An even deeper challenge is that, though modern American society *honors* heroes, it is not really a culture that strives to *create* them, or even knows how to deal with them once they appear. We are, after all, the nation that was urged to fight terrorism by being more confident consumers; we are taught, at levels from elementary school discipline to sophisticated consulting advice, to think in terms of cost and benefit. People might become soldiers or pursue other heroic careers out of a sense of national duty, the desire to be heroes. But it has been years since we automatically asked for that. The boomers grew up with "ask not what your country can do for you." The game generation, instead, got "be all you can be." (And even that has been recently upgraded to "an army of one"—presumably by the same recruiting command that authorized the creation of *America's Army,* "a highly realistic and innovative PC video game that puts you inside an Army unit. . . . Gain experience as a soldier in the U.S. Army, without ever leaving your desk."³) Political figures and celebrities do use some of their bully pulpit time to honor volunteers, people who achieve something important for society without much chance of personal benefit. But if our culture, from business to policy to entertainment, has delivered any single message during the entire lifetime of the game generation, it is this: People worth emulating end up reaping major material rewards. Respect belongs to those who earn success. And—to be painfully obvious—success equals money. Ideally, there should also be fame in the mix. But fame without money is, for us as a people, a peculiar and shameful type of failure; it means you had the chance to cash in, but somehow blew it. Just look at the jokes about Willie Nelson and his troubles with the IRS, or aging stars like MC Hammer and Gary Coleman descending to reality television.

Heroism may be natural for adolescents, but it is not natural at all for most organizations. So a young person out to be a hero doesn't always fit neatly into the enterprise. For decades now, businesses big enough to be professionally managed have been run as perhaps the only thing they really can be: bureaucracies. We mean that in the technical sense, of course, not the pejorative; we manage the rules and the structure, not the individual people. Managers in organizations of all kinds, some hardly larger than extended families, devote enormous energy to fine-tuning incentives, policies, and management metrics. In large organizations, managers automatically assume that employees are profit maximizers; they will compete and cooperate in response to the incentives that managers provide.

But heroes, even nascent ones, see incentives differently from the rest of us. You can't really analyze the would-be hero's behavior in economic terms. Think of the famous heroes of September 11, the firefighters. Does anyone believe they took those jobs as profit maximization? And kept them, even after real experience with danger and hardship and loss, because of the great retirement plan? What about the many of us who have chosen safer, easier jobs that—even so—bring both greater social status and more money: Is there any salary that would have driven us out of professional school and into the police academy?

Of course not. When you choose the hero's role, the decision is not fundamentally about money. It is also, at least for many, not really about the goal of being a hero. For most in heroic fields, it is instead about the *experience of being a hero*: of facing a challenge with real teeth, where the reward is partly service to some larger cause. Of course, people who respond to that challenge may also respond to conventional incentives. We suspect that, on the margin, they will pursue higher pay or better pension plans at least as keenly as the rest of us. But they won't be led by those incentives. It is the opportunity to be the hero that inspires them. However they perceive or express it, that opportunity for service, for accepting a dramatic personal challenge is what drives their most important decisions (to become and remain a firefighter, for instance) and inspires their highest performance. If managers understand those motivations and give game generation professionals the opportunity to become heroes, the resulting performance can actually *be* heroic.

Harnessing Their Potential

The drive for heroism—like all the game generation's values—is of much more than academic interest. Because the generation is so large, its values matter. The question is how best to harness them. Many of the classic techniques, the ones you have used until now, can probably help. But a lot has changed. To help the game generation really achieve the professional excellence they so deeply want, and that the rest of us so deeply need as we shift from working professionals to passive investors, we believe managers should follow five new principles specific to leading the game generation:

First, tap the gamers' instinct for heroism. The game generation is not composed entirely of heroes in the literal, FDNY sense. But its members do have a fundamentally heroic belief: that their personal performance matters to others. And they have the hero's appetite for a challenge that requires full attention. Meeting these needs—giving the potential heroes who work for you a challenge that will inspire extreme efforts—can unleash enormous commitment. Doing so is mainly a matter of perspective. Obviously, it's not possible to make debugging a database or crafting a market strategy as physically dangerous as entering a burning building, nor is it necessary. What is possible, and advisable, is framing these tasks as opportunities for heroism. One dot-com we worked with, for example, directly and publicly linked every employee's efforts to major corporate goals—which often included sheer survival. We're not talking about performance objectives for the annual review here; more like tribal ceremonies. Every few weeks, small teams stood in front of the company's entire top leadership, as well as members of all the other teams, and committed to a set of goals that had obvious impact on launching the next product, increasing revenue, or winning another round of venture capital. Before making these high-stakes promises, they first had to report, point by point, on whether they had achieved the goals set from the last round.

And every employee knew that, just five or six weeks later, she would be standing in the same room, facing the same bosses and colleagues and investors, announcing success or failure on today's promises—which were also clearly linked to goals that everyone in the company shared. Every employee could see, and knew that others could see, how his performance had helped the side or let it down. The result was that the *nature* of the task did not change (debugging the database was still debugging the database), but its *meaning* was radically transformed. The programmers, the customer service reps, even the overworked and underappreciated guys who kept the network running—everyone had a chance to be a hero, or to fail. It concentrated the mind wonderfully.

Of course, creating a whole new system might not be an option for your team, at least not yet. But every manager can provide opportunities for heroism, if only one-on-one. Find the tasks you really need done; frame them as dangerous (or at least difficult) and important—they probably are—and provide a clear opportunity for public praise or public failure. That's the kind of pressure gamers are looking for. They might not literally thank you for it, but they will reward you with an intensity hard to inspire any other way.

Second, don't let the superficial badges of culture mislead you. Remember the old fogies who thought men with long hair automatically couldn't be trusted? (Remember the naïve young boomers who thought they automatically *could?*) We boomers now have the chance to replicate the fogies' mistake, or to build on major assets that our less open-minded peers overlook. The challenge is seeing past the superficial details, the ones that only seem important. The insult represented by those details is as dramatic as it was back in the days of hippies and hardhats, but the details themselves are considerably more subtle. Having lived through the near-violent switch from crew cuts and neckties to long hair and bell-bottoms, and then slid gently into "business casual," boomers aren't about to be tripped up by such trivia as odd hair or clothing—not even piercings and tattoos. Where many boomers go astray, though, is in evaluating the new generation's attitudes. After all, we have earned the right to call ourselves experts. We have learned and practiced, since childhood, the fine art of teamwork. And if in the process we have become control freaks, it is because *real* experience has taught us that "if something needs to be done right, I had better do it myself." Ironically, by expressing these very same attitudes, the game generation can easily offend their more senior managers and colleagues. It can seem inappropriate, almost like grasping for a seniority they haven't earned—even as gamers strike their elders as immature in other dimensions.

Yet as we have seen, many of the core values of the game generation are not so very different from our own. The challenge—the fastest way we know to see through that deceptive veneer—is to remember what *can* be underneath a gamer's seemingly abrasive comments or behavior, then consciously set out to find it. Try to ignore what seems like arrogance, for example; watch closely, instead, for professional pride.

Third, use the game generation's "selfish" drives to inspire great performance. This is more than just filling the gamer's need to be a hero; it's appealing to pride instead of greed, or even instead of ambition. Again, conventional economic incentives never fail completely. But they are often not enough—especially in a tight economy, when big raises and expensive perks just aren't in the cards. And they are often less important than any of us think—including the gamers themselves. Managers need to understand that the game generation is not filled with the kind of people a think tank colleague of ours once called "walking ROI calculators." It *is* true that gamers want the rewards that go with achievement. Working around them, you might hear a lot about that. But they also want to actually achieve. It's what they're used to. They want to *be* experts, and they also want to be recognized for that status. When one of these employees asks for compensation that seems outrageous, listen to what's behind the talk of salary; what they really might be asking for is simply pride of place. And they might respond, much more than you expect, to a specific challenge to actually earn it.

Fourth, don't dismiss gamers' ability to concentrate and quickly move between tasks. In some cases, gamer employees will prefer to be surrounded by extraneous noise and attentional clutter. They might want to have two or three activities assigned to them at once so that when they tire of one, they can move to the next, and the come back to the first when they have something useful to add. Baby boomers were not trained to get things done this way. And we admit, from a purely cognitive point of view, that multitasking might not be the most efficient way to do things. But in terms of theoretical efficiency, it just doesn't matter as much as practical effectiveness. For young adults who were born into information-glut surroundings, it might be that a change is as good as a rest. Crazy as multitasking looks, it might even be difficult for the game generation to work hard any other way. And if you face tough group analytic problems—you do, don't you?—have some of your gamer-like employees try cutting-edge tools. You might not be comfortable with the tools themselves, but you might love the results.

Fifth, help your people work together across the generation gap. Video games might not be the social and psychological disaster that many have predicted over the years, but they *have* created a huge potential problem in teamwork. The problem is not gamers' inability to work in teams; it's the difficulty of establishing great teamwork between two generations that see each other as very different. Today, as in any era, different age groups have to work together. But bridging the generation gap is far more important at this particular moment in economic history. Precisely because gamers and boomers have grown up so differently, they have a great deal to offer each other professionally. Members of the game generation tend to bring intuitive technical skill, as well as problem-solving strategies and attitudes that just couldn't have evolved outside their digital world. Boomers, of course, have the lessons of experience—not to mention all the skills they honed during the time they were *not* playing digital games. By learning from one another, the two groups can make any organization far more capable. But the same generation gap that enables this dramatic learning can also create dramatic collisions. Any time disparate cultures meet, misunderstanding is possible. When the two cultures don't realize how different they are—when each group thinks that the other assumes the same principles and uses the same language—then those misunderstandings can be incredibly destructive.

To help your company avoid that kind of destruction, and capture instead the energy, wisdom, and problem-solving skills contained in these two groups, it is vital to build a bridge. Right now, as the two generations come together for what is really their first prolonged and broad-based contact, is the moment to knit the two professional cultures together. This is the time for boomers and gamers to see one another's differences, to understand what those differences really mean, and—most important—to recognize their deep similarities. Each generation has bonded internally over very different experiences. Each sees, on the surface, alarming traits in the other's professional attitudes. But both value skill, expertise, and results. Both care about the company. Both can amaze the other—and you—with their performance.

To help them see all that, you must make the first move: Provide an experience specifically designed to expose boomers' and gamers' differences and similarities in a controlled setting. You want them to see the dramatically different veneers of each group, and also the common values that lie beneath. You need them to discover the limits of their own skills, the value of the other group's different approach, and the operational tricks needed to tie the two together. And, if possible, you'd like them to invent a kind of common language—a set of experiences and problems they have to face together. This event becomes a touchstone they can go back to when they meet challenges in real life. In our experience, the fastest and most effective way to provide all that is through a task force or special project set off a little from the run of daily work life. A simulation might help here. But even better is to provide a real challenge. Working on a real task helps discourage political posturing and allows for frequent feedback to show what's working. It is especially good for helping two groups that don't naturally understand each other learn to perform together at a very high level. And learning to perform well with members of the *other* generation is the key to unlocking the game generation's potential as great professionals.

CHAPTER FIVE

Play Nice

AFTER ALL THAT TIME ALONE, CAN GAMERS
BE GREAT TEAM PLAYERS?

EVERY MANAGER WE KNOW wants employees who are competitive, good at solving problems, and at least a little driven. These are all qualities one can imagine learning from computer games. But every manager we know also wants people who have something more to offer. No matter how competitive the industry, you still need people who know how to collaborate. Even in a cutthroat star system, you need team players. When we began our research, we expected that in this aspect, if nowhere else, the game generation would fall short. After all, don't parents fear that their game-playing children will flunk the classic grade school measure, "works and plays well with others"? In its absorbing isolation, the game world looks almost misanthropic. On a deeper level, games reflect a very strange view of human society. Players spend most of their time interacting not with actual people, but with two-dimensional characters—almost cartoons.

It's not just the content; the very structure of the activity, the world that the games assume, and the principles they would seem to build deep into the players' psyches, are worrisome. Games don't seem to have anything to do with teamwork or community. The isolation even shows up in the physical design of the activity; whether it's played on a computer or a television or a handheld, in a remote corner of the house or in a busy family room, the game essentially demands that players orient their attention to *it*, not to other people. As with television, of course, players face the screen. But because games move more quickly, generally provide more visual information, and exact harsh penalties for any lapses of attention, players must watch the screen closely during the entire game. The controller, of course, occupies their hands, which are in a constant state of readiness, if not actual motion.

If a player wants to give you more than fragmentary attention, she has to stop playing the game; there's really no game equivalent of chatting while watching TV. And if you, the observer, want to follow the player's progress, you must track the objects and action on the screen—the digital display of the game—not the human playing it. Even while two players are interacting with each other, virtually all of their attention is on the screen and controllers and not on each other. And gamers are presumably focusing their attention on games instead of more traditional activities such as Little League, scouting, or sandlot sports—the kinds of activities in which our culture assumes we learn teamwork. It's no wonder parents worry.

There's simply no question about it; a lot of gaming does involve gamers' temporary withdrawal from the people around them, or at least from most of them. They might not be totally alone—but they often are.

Is that so bad? Absolutely not. Generations of American parents have invested serious money, serious amounts of their children's time, and even more serious angst in an equally artificial and solitary activity: piano lessons. It is shocking, we know, to compare the high-culture staple of piano lessons to the lowly video game. But there are surprising points of resemblance: arcane, highly complex finger movements; a huge premium on repetition in practice; and the difficulty of really sharing the experience with anyone who doesn't play. Perhaps the most important similarity is this: both are, in a certain way of thinking, self-centered. For most of us, neither piano nor video games are economically or even practically productive. They are hard to justify in any terms except our own pleasure at doing the activity. As many nonparticipants have observed, the quintessential business game, golf, is equally time-consuming and fruitless. From Mark Twain's "good walk spoiled" philosophy to the stereotypical golf widow, probably millions of people, including many golfers themselves, have wondered why anyone cares about hitting a little white ball over a great distance into a hole in the ground. Golfers will be quick to point out that there are reasons: the sound of the club scything through the air, the arc of a well-hit wood, the satisfying *thoint* of the ball dropping in the hole. But as with a video game, the only person who really feels these things is the person actually playing.

That separation is the point. Golf, like playing the piano or playing video games, is ours alone. In a world where our time, our goals, our skills, even our daily calendars are shared, we have an activity that no one else can really care about, and no one else can really even experience, but us. The golf course, the piano, and the video game are all places where, in the end, only we can go. Even when we are there with others, the deepest part of the experience is somewhere in our own minds. So we understand the attraction of this strange new world. But we must also face reality: If people spend *so* many hours in such a solitary environment—hundreds or thousands of hours at a formative age—wouldn't you expect them to be a little less connected to the rest of us?

Gamers Like People

That lack of connection is certainly what many expect. But there must be more going on in games than what we boomers see. Our survey made it very clear: Gamers are *not* isolated, introverted, or unsociable. In general, they care about other people exactly as much as the rest of us do. When presented with the statement, "I find people more stimulating than anything else," members of this generation answered with boringly similar levels of agreement. The average level of agreement for the game generation as a whole is slightly lower than for the older generation represented in our survey. But within the game generation, gamers seem to be slightly more people-oriented (or maybe people-stimulated) than those who didn't play games growing up. When we look at all the respondents born before the game generation, the difference between the most frequent gamers and those who didn't game at all is very small. Even more telling, this data suggests that frequent gamers are at least as stimulated by people as moderate gamers or those who never play at all. So parents' unspoken but deep-seated fear that video games might turn their children into loners finds no support in the data.

This finding—the lack of evidence supporting the loner myth—is surprising enough. But for a prospective employer, colleague, or investor, the news about the game generation gets even better. In this huge and important age group, there is a clear trend suggesting that *the more time young professionals have spent playing video games, the more sociable they report themselves to be.* This trend shows up in survey questions that measure what psychologists usually call "relatedness needs." To analyze this trait statistically, psychologists ask respondents to agree or disagree with statements such as, "Being accepted and appreciated by coworkers, having close friends at work, is important." The game generation, on average, is *more* likely than previous cohorts to agree with these statements. That is, they have a greater need for relatedness than boomers and other groups that have dominated the workforce until now. Even more interesting, within the game generation, respondents with more gaming experience have higher scores on this measure of need for relationships with other people. The difference is small but statistically significant, and the pattern is very clear. Nongamers express the lowest average need for others' companionship at work; moderate gamers are in the middle; and those with frequent gaming experience (past or present) express this need most often. The picture among older respondents is equally clear and quite significant: Those who played games as kids express higher needs for good and strong relationships than those who did not. Of course nothing about the survey can demonstrate causality; we don't know from this data whether more sociable people sought out games, or whether games made otherwise average people more sociable. What we do know is that if someone you hire has lots of digital game experience, your safest bet is that she will place *more* value on the team around her, not less.

The most important finding here is that, where we might have expected to find isolation, the data instead reveals that gamers care more, not less, about connecting with other people. The game generation, on average, is more likely than previous cohorts to want to be accepted. Within the game generation, respondents with more gaming experience need relationships with other people more often. In addition, our survey found that these connections are a big part of why they game in the first place: Roughly half of gamers say they play as a social experience.

To a nongamer, the possibility that gaming can be social is not at all intuitive. But once the question is raised, it's easy to see that presumably isolating video games can actually be quite social. *EverQuest*, for example, takes place in a far-off fantasy world. Within that setting, it lets you play with many others, people you probably don't know in any other context, collaborating and competing at the same time to build up your own level of experience. How different is that from the generic description of a business career? Other social themes far beyond the stereotypes of *anime*, witchcraft, and space opera are also attracting gamers. Sysis, a company that develops "online artificial life simulations," created an online dating game called *Flirtboat*, in which players register to play one of four three-month games, creating a virtual character who will live out a virtual life on the Web while the real person gets on with his life offline. The players on *Flirtboat* build up points by the way they interact and flirt with other virtual characters.

These games are literally social; tens of thousands of players can be logged onto a single MMPORPG at any one time, and the characters interacting in *Flirtboat* are in some sense simply proxies for real human beings. But pure single-player games can also have a strong social element. In *Creatures*, an elaboration on those keychain virtual pets called "Tamagotchi," players raise a creature from the moment it hatches—feeding and caring for it, teaching it to get along with others, punishing it when it's bad. In *Black and White*, each player's treatment of the monster she raises determines if that monster will become good or evil. The comparison to childrearing is obvious, though parents would point out that—as is so often true in games—the real life version is a little more complicated.

One of PC gaming's biggest hits ever has been *The Sims,* a soap-opera-like setting in which players can decorate a home, have a career, and fall in love. A ten-year-old girl we'll call Sarah, for example, plays *The Sims* for a couple of hours a day. She has created neighborhoods of families that interact with each other and imbued them with qualities that she finds interesting. Because she's played so much, Sarah has figured out the logic underlying the program—the set of relationships that might relate personality characteristics and activities to general wealth-building in this game. In one case, she had developed a family that she dearly loved. They were nice, loving, caring people—good neighbors, good parents, very family-centered. But she could see that they were never going to get rich and live in a great home. So Sarah hatched a devious plan. She created a new family in the neighborhood with all the characteristics that she thought would yield high wealth. They were not necessarily likeable people. She wanted them to build and appoint a beautiful home—a mansion. And she wanted them to do it quickly. The family took on very high debt to build the house. Then Sarah made sure they kept spending and spending and spending. Finally, the family with the beautiful home had to declare bankruptcy and the house was put up for auction.

Here's where it gets really good. Sarah then made sure that her nice family was the only one that bid on the home when it came up for auction. They were able to move into the great house for a song and they still remained a nice family. No big deal, right—pretty much what you (and we) were doing at age ten?

In another life lesson, Sarah set up one household that was inhabited by a gay couple. She did everything she could to make sure that the guys were happy in their lives, but was frustrated by the limitations of the game itself. She finally went to her dad to see if he could fix the flaw with the computer. As soon as she explained the problem, he saw that his daughter wasn't dealing with a computer bug; she was learning about society and unreasonable laws. Sarah wanted her gay couple to get married, but the game at that time wouldn't allow it.

The hidden element of teamwork—sometimes with other people in the same room, sometimes with other players online, and sometimes with characters who, strictly speaking, don't exist at all—might explain why the isolation, the lack of team spirit, that many expect from game playing simply didn't pan out in real life. No matter what it looks like to outsiders, it appears that to those who take part in it, gaming does not feel like a solitary pursuit. Tens of millions of people log on every day to game portals such as Microsoft's Zone.com and Yahoo! Games, paying to subscribe to game playing services that give them the chance to win cash and prizes. Some games attract such broad demographics—including droves of women and older players—that major companies such as Intel and McDonald's are looking to get their products inserted into the games. To parents who worry about unsocialized offspring, or managers who wonder whether their new employees will be able to work together, that broadening of gaming's appeal is at least somewhat reassuring. At a minimum, it means that our innate drive to interact with others still functions. It might even mean that real social interaction is still taking place even though the players look, to nongamers, like they are in a trance.

Training Ground

Even though current video games can provide a lot of interaction with fellow humans, the depth of that interaction can only be called perfunctory. But, as it turns out, that superficial experience does not make games unsocial, or unimportant socially. It actually makes gamers more experienced team members. How can that be?

To begin, games always provide structure—rules, competition, turns, and so forth. With digital games, those structures tend to be more confining (because of the interface, some things are just too hard to do) and a bit formulaic (though there are thousands of game titles, the number of really distinct genres, or even game plots, is quite small). Not even the most sociable, realistic, high-fidelity game we can imagine is all that much like real life with real humans. The whole point of playing games is to make some aspect of real life conveniently, unrealistically simple. Social games certainly succeed on that score.

Their structured nature is perhaps why games have produced a generation that in business terms is so enthusiasti-
cally social. They have given players hundreds of chances
to work together (either with actual humans or with human-
designed characters) in a structured setting, as opposed to
just hanging out or talking about work. As many of us have
discovered in professional life, the art of working together is
social, but it is far different from the unstructured sociability
of interacting without a defined goal. Computer and video
games actually provide a specific and important—if somewhat odd—framework for socialization. They provide a way
to create and deepen social relationships by using a limited,
nearly impersonal goal. Gamers will create their own unique
techniques for interacting based on the games they grew up
with. The business professionals who can successfully understand those techniques will find themselves discovering
unexpected benefits. The social aspects of gaming may not be
socialization as boomers knew it, but they may be much more
relevant for the social life of organizations.

So Now What, Einstein?

To see what we mean, spend a few moments playing Einstein. That is, conduct a small thought-experiment, as Einstein
liked to do; only instead of railroad cars and cats, use subjects
from your own company. Imagine a group of managers
whose work intersects, but whose organizational perspec-
tives are very different—something like a new product development team that includes representatives from marketing,
R&D, operations, and accounting. In the first trial, put this
group in a room with no agenda at all—say, at an office party.
They certainly won't produce anything. They probably won't

even talk to each other; instead, they'll break up into the same groups that normally work together. In the second trial, place the same participants in a meeting where they are to discuss the issues that arise in new product development. This time, you'll probably get some output, but much of it will be complaints that you have heard before. In the third and final trial, put the same players into a strategy game where they simulate getting a new product to market. This time, wouldn't you expect real results? The product might not be any good, but the process is likely to produce real value: genuine insights, new ways of working together, and maybe even solutions to internal problems that you had assumed would never be resolved.

This thought-experiment reveals why games, which seem at first to be isolating, can actually teach the kind of social attitudes needed in business. All three of our imaginary trials involved social activities among coworkers, but the most purely social activity had the *least* social impact. It failed to advance the relationships that are probably most important to your company's success. The most structured and artificial exercise, on the other hand, did a great deal to improve the group's shared capabilities. As social interactions go, games are limited, even distorted. But so is business. It may be these very flaws—games' artificial structure and their narrow scope—that prepare gamers to work together in a focused and productive way.

Tough Cookies

We don't mean to imply that gamers are perfect employees, or the most easygoing players your team will ever have. Our research found that members of the game generation are inclined to make their wishes known immediately and often. Compared to older respondents, the average member of the game generation is more likely to acknowledge that "I strive to be in control of the group." Boomers are infamous for wanting it all. Gamers, in contrast, want it their way, and they want it now.

In our survey we also found that gamers can be emotionally volatile. By their own estimate, they are more likely than other groups to be easily annoyed or upset. In a word, they can be irritable. The good news is that this trait, at least in the extreme form measured by this survey, only affects a minority of the cohort. Even in the most irritable subset (young respondents who played games frequently as teenagers), only 20 percent rated themselves as easily annoyed or upset. But that number is noticeably higher than for peers who played games less often. The entire game generation, both on average and by game-frequency category, is much more emotionally volatile than baby boomers or other cohorts. As figure 5-1 makes clear, respondents from each experience

FIGURE 5-1

Emotionality: I Get Upset Easily; Many Things Annoy Me; I Often Feel Insecure; I Am Quick Tempered

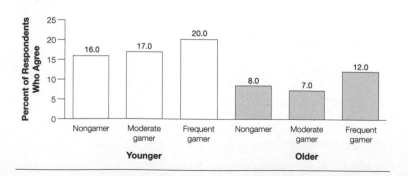

group within the game generation are about twice as likely as their older counterparts to rate themselves highly on these irritability scores.

Surly Dogs

Although they want to be part of the team, members of the game generation also seem somewhere between realistic and cynical about how that team and its members work. A huge majority believe that "generally speaking, people won't work hard unless they are forced to do so." Frequent gamers are noticeably more likely to argue that "connecting with the right people is how to get things done" (see figure 5-2). The more gaming experience they have, the more likely respondents are to agree with more extreme statements as well, including, "I would go out of my way to make friends with powerful people" and "the best way to handle people is to tell

FIGURE 5-2

The Best Way to Get Things Done Is to Connect with the Right People

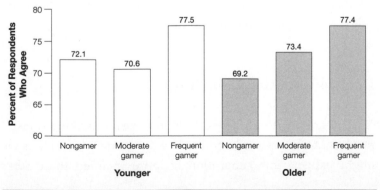

them what they want to hear." To be clear, these Machiavellian attitudes extend to the gamers' view of themselves. It's almost as if they see work life as a game, and themselves as skillful players. In that model, other people might come across as both needing direction and essentially inviting manipulation. So it would not surprise us that people with this background might see themselves as capable of providing that manipulation. A strong majority of the game generation agrees with the statement, "I can control the way I come across to people, depending on the impression I wish to make."

Whether or not these attitudes are desirable in team members is a judgment call; presumably, it depends somewhat on the particular team in question. What is undeniable, though, is that these are attitudes of people who care about being effective in team situations—about working through and with others to achieve goals—and who in fact are investing themselves in understanding how to do that.

We see this orientation not only in the attitudes toward teamwork explored earlier, but also in the game generation's decision-making style. Gamers, like other groups, follow a variety of patterns in making business decisions. *But the clear, common thread is that—more than one would expect—they are more skilled than nongamers at using a wide range of tactics to involve other people in making decisions.*

Decision Making *à la* Group

Their tendency to involve others in decision making doesn't mean that gamers see business as a democracy. In fact, as we might expect, this generation is more inclined than other groups to take the reins personally. Most members of the game generation agree with the statement, "I prefer to be responsible for most decisions for my work group and me." (This attitude is also a classic measure of entrepreneurial tendencies; it's no surprise, then, that the generation that provided raw horsepower for all those dot-coms would score high.) Older respondents are more likely to agree. Their agreement probably has to do with their naturally higher level of experience and confidence, not to mention our hierarchical expectation that older people will be the ones to make the decisions. In both age groups, the more gaming experience you have, the more likely you are to take on the ultimate responsibility for decisions.

So far, these results are what one would expect: The confident and controlling gamers we've seen automatically assume that they'll be calling the shots. But here is where things get social—and interesting. When we look at the process that respondents choose for calling those shots, *the game generation seems surprisingly inclined, and fluidly able, to involve their subordinates in decision making.*

Years of research in leadership and organizational behavior have confirmed what most of us have experienced in practical business life: Effective leaders take responsibility for decisions, but get substantial input from the members of their teams. There are moments, of course, when a more authoritarian model is needed; the leader simply has to make the call, and input from others would not help. There are even times at the egalitarian end of the scale, when it's best to have the group make the decision as a whole. But as a rule, effective managers tend toward decision-making styles between those two extremes. They know that the information and insights from the group are vital, so involving employees should be almost automatic. They also know that for speed, coherence, and leadership, the buck actually does have to stop somewhere. This balance is especially vital for any organization that needs to be smart but also nimble.

The need for balance between the extremes of decision-making styles seems obvious. Even organizations with more classically rigid and authoritarian decision-making styles, such as the military or very large companies, have spent enormous effort over the past decades training managers to achieve that magic balance. Those organizations should be thrilled, then, to find that the generation they are now largely hiring from seems to strive for that same magic balance automatically.

Our survey asked respondents how comfortable they were with each of five decision-making styles, ranging from quite authoritarian to quite egalitarian. (For this measure, the research team adapted survey questions traditionally used for the Vroom-Yetton Model, also known as the Normative Model, a model of managerial decision making introduced in 1973 that is widely used to analyze the extent to which leaders should involve subordinates in the decision-making process.[1]) The results were as follows:

- The game generation was less authoritarian than previous cohorts (the ones who have been through all that training to help improve their leadership styles).
- The rising cohort was far more comfortable with decision-making styles that balance the leader's authority with significant input from subordinates.
- The most frequent gamers generally led in their comfort with all the balanced decision styles.

"Who's the Boss?"

Less than ten percent of the gamers we asked said they would be comfortable with "making the decision on their own without discussing it with employees under their supervision." This style was also relatively unpopular with boomers and other pregame generations, though they were a little more likely to prefer it. Within the game generation, there seems to be no clear relationship between gaming experience and comfort with authoritarian decision making. Nongamers were a little more comfortable than frequent gamers with this model, and moderate gamers were least comfortable of all. However, older gamers may really be as different from their peers as those old stereotypes suggest, since respondents with the most gaming experience were noticeably more likely to prefer the authoritarian style.

"Don't Worry Your Pretty Little Head About It"

The same trend continues when we ask about a decision-making style that is a bit more egalitarian, yet still clearly authoritarian: the manager who "asks for information from the employees he or she supervises, but makes the decision on his or her own without necessarily sharing the details of the problem with them."

This decision-making style, which jaded employees might call the mushroom school of management (because the employee is kept in the dark and provided with an extremely rich—and pungent—culture medium), is slightly more appealing to the game generation than the pure command mode—but not much. As with the authoritarian style, we see that the older groups are more likely to use this model than gamers are, and that the older frequent gamers are most enthusiastic of all.

"Information Wants to Be Free"

Once the survey begins to cover more egalitarian decision-making styles (the ones around that magic balance point), the pattern becomes even stronger. When the approach is described as "share the problem one-on-one with employees and ask for their input, but make the decision on your own," the game generation's comfort level goes up dramatically (see figure 5-3). The most experienced gamers in this age group are nearly twice as likely to choose this leadership style than a more authoritarian style. So members of the game generation—especially frequent gamers—are much more comfortable with involving others in making decisions.

FIGURE 5-3

The Best Way to Make a Decision Is to Share the Problem One-on-One with Employees and Ask for Their Input, but Make the Decision on My Own

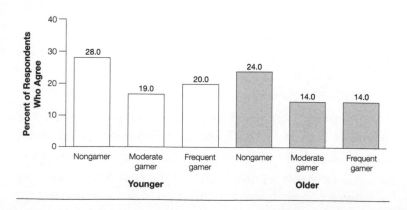

"Let's Talk About This"

When asked about a leadership style that has the same balance of power but relies on group meetings, an interesting difference emerges. The game generation's response to this leadership style ("meet with employees as a group to discuss the problem, but make the decision on your own") is almost exactly the same as to the previous style. That is, they are equally comfortable getting subordinates' input one-on-one or in a group. The older cohorts, in contrast, are significantly more likely to prefer the group meeting model. This is especially true for moderate gamers and those with no gaming experience. To anyone who sees more than enough meetings on the corporate calendar, this is a clear edge for the game generation; managers who can lead a team without constant meetings will, all other things being equal, get more done faster. It might also reflect a stronger entrepreneurial tendency (calling a group meeting sends a strong signal that employees were consulted; getting input one-on-one is, in a sense, a more confident and decisive model), or simply a tendency to see many different ways to communicate with the team, versus a rigid choice between one-on-one communication and meetings.

"The Age of Aquarius"

Whatever drives the game generation's balanced leadership style, it is clearly not a preference for group decisions above all else. The game generation is still reasonably comfortable with the option of "meet with employees as a group to discuss the problem and have the group make the decision." But all in all the generation is less comfortable with this egalitarian model than with the more balanced styles.

This drop is sharpest among the most experienced gamers, who are about 20 percent less likely to be comfortable with pure group decisions than with their own decisions based on group input. That drop for frequent gamers mirrors the reaction of all members of the older cohorts. On this item we see yet again that *young professionals with extensive gaming experience display the same attitudes as much more experienced managers.* And that similarity, in a sense, is the strongest message from all the items on leadership style. Technically, young gamers' preferences on leadership style are interesting, even quite encouraging. The rising generation of managers is a little less authoritarian than previous cohorts and much more comfortable with decision styles that include significant input from subordinates. They're comfortable getting that input in just about any format. All these attributes are great, for organizations and for the game generation's prospects. But the really striking message is that, with teamwork as with other professional attitudes, the game generation seems to have somehow accumulated experience beyond their years. Yes, games have let them be the boss far earlier and more often than real life allows. In the *Madden Football* series (to take an incredibly popular example from a milieu that is— how shall we say?—not famously intellectual), you're the owner, general manager, coach, *and* quarterback of any football team you want. Strategy games tend to place you as Alexander the Great, not one of those nameless guys down in the phalanx. And the entire experience is almost always under your control. That's unrealistic, but it might be why, as a group, gamers come into the workforce already preferring leadership styles that corporations often spend years training for—and why those with the most gaming experience show the strongest results. Maybe emulating the boss brings lessons as well as virtual perks.

They Can All Just Get Along

No matter how skilled the game generation seems to be, their full potential for teamwork won't be realized automatically on entering the workforce. To the boomers around and above them, gamers might not look like the enthusiastic team players that they really are. And their social skills—developed as they were in a structured, high technology environment— might not fit instantly into more traditional corporate cultures. Today's managers and executives could, of course, simply leave it to the gamers themselves to adapt; after all, we were here first. But given how large the game generation is, how independent and entrepreneurial it has already proven to be in fueling the dot-coms, and how much potential it offers not only to meet but to surpass today's performance standards, asking the gamers to do all the adapting seems like a mistake. Instead, why not be the first to capture an untapped resource? To make the most of this generation's innate sociability, executives only need to consider three types of possible changes:

First, provide a little structure. Remember, professionals from this generation have already spent hundreds or thousands of their socialization hours in clearly defined, goal-directed tasks. And they chose that kind of environment voluntarily, often in the face of significant parental disapproval. It is presumably the social setting they prefer, or at least feel comfortable in. So in situations in which you want to create stronger relationships that include this generation, do what you can to replicate and leverage that familiar structure. Doing so doesn't mean converting your workplace to a video arcade. But it does mean that small talk and many traditional team-building exercises won't work as well for this large and rising group as activities with a little more shape. Games themselves would be better than cocktail parties. Special projects, real or simulated (like the war games we discuss in chapter 7), would be better yet. As we'll see in the next chapter, gamers value performance, in themselves and in others. Give them chances to bond over successful projects. Even if those projects don't seem "real" to you, they will add more to your company's capabilities than the glow of a company picnic—and last longer, too.

Second, help them learn local standards. As in other areas, small social things can divide this generation from the rest of us in a destructive and completely unnecessary way. Not only have gamers spent more social time in structured, almost work-like settings than we did, but they also have a very different experience with technology and the behaviors it makes possible (or even sensible). Instant messaging is a great example. For many of us who came to computers as adults, the screen and keyboard feel like a private space—a place we go to do actual work, not to conduct meetings or to be entertained. This generation, of course, sees digital environments as simply additional parts of the everyday world. For your established workers who are boomers, when an instant message pops up on the screen, it's a rude and distracting interruption. But for gamers, who have grown up socializing with and through the computer screen, the same IM is not only a sensible way to interact; it is such a great productivity aid that not using it would be clueless, almost criminal. There will be other examples, some involving technology itself, others more purely about behavior. We've seen, for instance, that multitasking is quite common among gamers. Yet for their elders, doing two things at once seems almost disrespectful; it means you're not all that serious about either. Neither attitude is necessarily wrong. But these generational differences can be destructive if unrecognized. Or they can be *productive* if both groups understand the ground rules. Your role is simply to be alert to such issues and to make sure they are addressed. You might also consider setting up two-way mentor relationships in which the technologically savvy but structure-dependent gamers learn some of the things they might not have had time for—such as how to conduct small talk on a sales call—while perhaps passing along some of the digital expertise they seem to have been born with. The game generation might not need traditional social skills with each other, but colleagues and customers from earlier generations will notice the difference and appreciate it.

Third, manage your teams as group video games. Don't worry, you don't have to provide magic potions or X-wing fighters. What you should do, to get the most out of game generation employees, is provide the kind of team environment where they will automatically be motivated and productive. That environment begins with how you structure the work— the equivalent of game design. Structure team assignments like a game, providing clear high-level direction but also lots of room to explore. Tell your team, "Here are the boundaries; you can't go outside them, but inside try anything—open all the doors, run into the walls, find a way to succeed." Providing a productive environment for the game generation extends through how you react to the unexpected; gamers *will* do things you've never envisioned. Let them! (As long as they don't violate those few really crucial boundaries.)

Remember, it was members of this generation who, in the interactive game *EverQuest*, hacked the system to allow them to create (and wear) a fluorescent pink suit of armor. There had always been a choice of traditionally "knightly" colors available—but shocking pink was not on the menu. It is not surprising that, on seeing a player arrayed in bright pink armor, other people wanted it, too. And once the gamers wanted the pink armor, they were willing to barter, beg, or buy the right to sport those steel togs. A black market even emerged; the code for the pink armor was being hawked on eBay for hundreds of dollars. In the end, no harm, no foul. The game generation had explored every nook and cranny of the *EverQuest* game and found a way to make a market out of something no one had ever expected would sell. Give gamers some rein to explore your company, your industry, your customer segment, and see if they don't use that same creative streak to add value to your organization.

CHAPTER SIX

Win or Go Home

HOW VIDEO GAMES BUILT ROI INTO THIS GENERATION'S DNA

GAMERS DON'T JUST LEARN about people; all that gaming experience teaches them about the rest of reality, too. Games show them how the world works. One of the strongest lessons they learn is also potentially one of the most troublesome, or perhaps the most exciting: Gamers learn that *failure doesn't hurt.* A Nintendo GameCube ad in shopping malls, for example, confronts teens with an oversized X ray of a human torso, highlighting an enormous steel plate and multiple screws that seem to be holding the arm together. The caption reads "359°." The implication is that for extreme types cool enough to play GameCube, real-world 360s, on skateboards or snowboards or some technology the rest of us haven't even heard of, are a routine fact of life, and if the price for missing one is hours of pain, major surgery, and maybe a little less mobility for the next sixty years or so, that's just life on the digital edge.

Our data don't cover physical risk, but there is reason to believe that gamers are emotionally tough. Although they don't talk about it much, failure is a huge part of the gaming experience. Before winning most games, they will have failed hundreds of times. Such high failure rates can be extremely productive. Because of the probability of failure, players naturally focus on what they did wrong, what they could have done better, and how they can get to the next level. So the game generation learns through repetition something that countless team coaches have tried to instill: Failure is part of the process that leads to success.

You can see this perspective in gamers' typical reactions to the dot-com bubble. Both gamers and boomers (the latter often in the role of "adult supervisors") took similar risks and had similar hopes. But their deepest assumptions—the ones each group took for granted—were vastly different. To a baby boomer from the professional classes, economic life is supposed to bring both security and rising wealth. God or Adam Smith or Louis Rukeyser set it up that way. No matter what we boomers might say about understanding the risks, we know that ordinary companies are not supposed to crash and burn. That kind of failure is only for dramatic exceptions, not for *our* employers and *our* investments. But to the game generation, risk is real and natural. It includes extreme consequences. And it is the inevitable, acceptable price of seeking any success worth the name. In other words, the game generation actually believes the risk/reward rhetoric that the rest of us just parrot when business school classes or SEC regulations or our hyperrational consciences require us to.

Unfortunately, what the game generation might not understand, even now, is that failure in the game world just doesn't hurt as much as the failure we older folks are more familiar with. There is no physical element to failing at a video game, of course. But there is also much less social pain.

That lack of social stigma is partly a matter of isolation; if you've got to pay your digital dues by crashing, or dying, or floundering, at least you can do it in the privacy of your own house or even your own room. It's also partly a matter of the lack of live competitors; if you lose in most sports, you lose *to* someone or even to a group of someones. Videogames let you move through those awkward stages losing only to a digital opponent. Perhaps it's natural, then, that by traditional standards, the game generation takes pain and failure less seriously. In any event, their attitude toward failure allows them to accept more risk, because from their perspective the risk is just part of the game. Some would argue that if real-life experiments such as the dot-com bubble are any indication, the game generation has absorbed the lesson too well.

Risky Business

Whether the game generation takes risk too naturally, of course, is a matter of interpretation. What can't be denied is that, as a group, gamers have different attitudes toward risk than the rest of us. Compared to those who play less often, frequent gamers are much more likely to agree that "taking measured risks is the best way to get ahead." Within the game generation, those who played frequently as teens are more likely to agree with that statement than their age-mates who played moderately or not at all. (The pattern is similar for older populations.) The same holds true for a different statement: "The best rewards come to people who take risks" (see figure 6-1).

This appetite for risk seems like a natural outgrowth of the way this generation has grown up. As a cynical boomer might

FIGURE 6-1

The Best Rewards Come to Those Who Take Risks

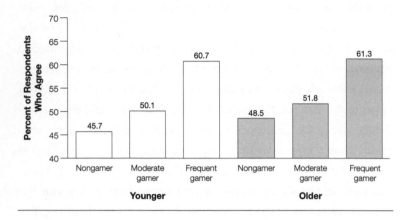

put it, "If they had spent more time out here and less time in there, they might be a little more cautious." To be clear, our national survey does not depict this generation as reckless. But it does reveal that gamers are more comfortable with risk than other groups. They believe it is important, and they are willing to accept it. Both attitudes align perfectly with the reality, so to speak, found in digital games. The games reward risk, of course, because without trying something new, you don't advance through the game. There is generally a limit; as in real life, some risks turn out to be foolish. But, comparing game reality to the more conventional kind, that limit seems to be set high. And the limit at the other end—the lowest amount of risk that leads to an acceptable outcome—seems high as well. The result is that the norm gamers experience as they play is to take more dramatic risks than most people do outside the digital world. They learn that you have to take risks to succeed, that everyone takes them, and that ultimately all risks are survivable.

Comfortable, But Not Too Comfortable

These lessons have concrete and measurable effects which seem quite promising for business. *Gamers embrace risk for exactly the right business reasons.* Handling risk is crucial for leaders. There is almost always enormous room to disagree over how much risk to take, and how to take it. But the fundamental strategy is not open for discussion. It is axiomatic. There is exactly one legitimate reason to take business risk: to capture an appropriately large reward. Failing to recognize this trade-off and pursue the right rewards can get CEOs fired. So can taking on risk for any other reason.

The risk/reward trade-off is almost painfully obvious. But as a more seasoned manager might say, not everyone talking about risk is actually willing to take much of it. Gamers, however, are more likely to embrace risk than others are and for the appropriate reasons. As we saw earlier, game experience teaches about risk/reward trade-offs as relentlessly as the beginning investor course at a community college. And our survey discovered that, in a world where most people aren't up to taking risks, even in theory, gamers are dramatically better at it.

That's because gamers—like good senior executives—aren't looking for comfort and safety; they are after bigger prey. Presented with the statement, "My life is very secure and comfortable—the way I like it," gamers are less likely than other groups to agree. And frequent gamers who are members of this new generation agree the least often. That makes millions more of them eligible for the next phase of executive qualification: actually taking risk. As we see in figure 6-2, frequent gamers are significantly more likely than other groups to agree that "taking measured risks is the best way to get ahead."

FIGURE 6-2

Taking Measured Risks Is the Best Way to Get Ahead

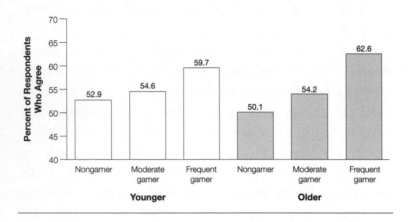

Taking measured risks to get ahead might not sound like a great leap. But remember: Many people don't agree with this seemingly tautological statement. Roughly half of professional respondents are looking for other ways to get ahead. That's one reason leaders and innovators and entrepreneurs are hard to find. The good news is that nearly two-thirds of frequent gamers agree that the goal is to find and take the right risks. This figure is clearly higher than for nongamers and those with moderate gaming experience. The levels are slightly higher for the older group, presumably because over time, experience teaches what executives take for granted. But because typical members of the game generation (moderate gamers) have more simulated experience, they are more likely to seek measured risks in business than typical boomers (nongamers), even with boomers' greater overall experience.

Of course, with NASDAQ losses still fresh on our brokerage statements, many of us might ask about the other side of taking risks. This generation is willing to embrace risk, but are they willing to stop? Thus the third test for executive-suite risk takers is: Do they care about avoiding it when they can? Or are they just a bunch of unseasoned daredevils?

These are reasonable questions. But the data presents surprisingly encouraging answers. Games don't reward unnecessary risk. And that experience seems to stick with gamers, because they are not interested in taking risks for the wrong reasons. The survey shows that *gamers are explicitly not thrill seekers.* There are people in every generation who take on risk purely for the emotional thrill. One might expect games, with their constant drive toward immersion and realistic excitement, to attract thrill-seekers, or perhaps even to produce more of them. But it appears that gamers are no more likely than other groups to have this characteristic.

Take the survey question, "The most important thing in life is fully experiencing all emotions." Our survey did not show any clear pattern of variation related to gaming experience in the responses. In both the older and younger populations, the range of variation is fairly small, and agreement does not consistently go up with game experience. Within the game generation, moderate gamers are more likely to agree than frequent gamers are. In the older group, that pattern is reversed; older nongamers are more likely than those with moderate experience to agree with this measure of risk taking for reasons beyond concrete reward. The younger population does score higher on this dimension than the older group does, but that is almost surely a pure age effect. The most important point here is the pattern that does *not* appear. On so many other dimensions, we have seen clear, dramatic trends in the data that link increasing game experience with the tendency being measured. The lack of that pattern here is telling. The safest conclusion seems to be that some gamers are surely thrill seekers, but gamers as a whole are not. They are willing to take risk, but not for the emotional punch—only for the right reward.

Are They Experienced?

As gamers begin to take risks for the rest of us, we need them to have not only the right attitude, but also the right kind of experience. Isn't experience something you want in an executive, a board member, even a boss? Here, the prospects are more worrisome. These future leaders have grown up in a world that *feels* wild, but is really artificial. Some would grumble that games look extreme but are really just kiddie rides. You may feel you're exploring outer space, but in truth, you are never farther than Tomorrowland.

Such statements are ironic, coming from baby boomers. The boomers' dominant medium, TV, is no better. The difference is in how the two are experienced. As the boomers were growing up, they couldn't confuse TV with reality; the technology just wasn't that powerful. Even today, with digital content on huge screens with multichannel sound, you're still just watching. With games, you're inside. Games aren't realistic. They're not even as high-fidelity as a good movie. Yet they feel like real life. They're complicated and hard; they respond to you; they *force* you to do something. In our experience it is impossible to play a game for more than a minute or two unless you're really trying. Otherwise, you're compelled to throw down the controller and rejoin the real world. Compare that experience to watching TV: We know the crisis will be resolved with or without us. We know we can catch up. So our attention drifts. Watch any proficient gamer play. How is that interaction being stored away in his memory? Is it just another image in his vast personal video archive? Or is it processed and internalized and subconsciously remembered as experience?

Yet whereas games feel like an experience, and may even *be* one, they're not quite like life in the real world. Most obviously, they're scripted. For example, you can run off the road while driving in *Need for Speed*. You can even have a wreck. Yet it seems impossible to total your car, much less injure yourself. In *Spiderman*, you get all the cool comic-book powers, but not all that much freedom. Basically, you can replicate the tasks of the movie, in order, or perform those variants that the designers happen to have thought of, or quit. Events are only unpredictable in ways that help the game. *Civilization* lets players take command of entire empires, but there is a generally agreed-upon rule of play that all rules are decided in advance; no war crimes here. And where there *is* unpredictability, it's the kind created by a decision tree and a random-number generator. It has only been in the past few years, in rare titles such as *I'm Going In*, that computer games have begun to simulate characters who behave with human inconsistency. What is the difference? Think about predicting a roll of the dice. Now think about what problem your most troublesome employee will come up with next. Most striking to us (after years in organizations in which very smart people attack the always humbling problem of predicting the future), the game world can't really provide unanticipated consequences. They may be unanticipated by the *player*—though not for long, if she's paying attention—but they can't be unanticipated by the *designer*. Real life is full of curveballs; the game world mainly throws regular pitches faster and faster.

All that predictable unpredictability could change. It might be possible to create real-life unpredictability; MMPORPGs, because they are driven by real humans playing roles, are an obvious place to start. But the defining reality of games—the common framework of goals, scoring systems, and a few standard if bizarre-looking interfaces—provides real limits. The larger barrier is created by gamers themselves. Would they really want a game as unstructured and unpredictable as life? Games are for fun. We consumers choose sheltered environments because we know they deliver fun in a safe package. It's the same reason that millions pay to ride roller coasters (which are intense and surprising but ultimately predictable and safe), yet would never agree to drive an unreliable old truck down crumbling mountain roads (which might not be scary at all, or on the other hand might actually be deadly).

So games are sheltered, not as wild and unpredictable as nature or business. So what? Haven't we said that a training-wheels environment is just the place for learning business skills?

Well, yes. But it's not the only place you need if what you want is to learn about running things. All that simulated experience, in so many sophisticated—but virtual—settings, might provide tactical lessons and even resilience for solving problems. (As one young manager told us, "People who have played games are a lot more creative and innovative and find solutions a little bit better instead of the whole following-procedures thing. There is something inherent in playing games . . . 'If this doesn't work I'll try it this way, if I'm stuck in the maze I'll try this.' You're in a situation for a reason, you're not usually stuck, so let's find a way around it, let's solve this problem.") Yet along with this skill and confidence comes a risk: expecting the relatively simple models found in games to represent real life. (After all, you can run a family in *The Sims* by attending to perhaps two dozen variables; in a real family, you would face literally thousands.)

Although games make it more common, expecting real life to be like models is hardly a new problem; it's the classic danger that surrounds freshly minted leaders, whether they are new lieutenants or new MBAs, making their first decisions outside the classroom. Officers or managers seasoned "on the battlefield" have a more complex set of models in their heads, they have developed judgment, and perhaps most important, they know that executing a strategy is harder than simply stating it. New leaders without ambiguous, messy experience miss those lessons, and often don't realize it. On paper, for example, this generation is financially sophisticated. But as the chairman of Oppenheimer Funds has observed, "Savings and investing-wise, single Gen X women are where women in general were a decade ago—increasingly empowered and aware but not doing what they should,"[1] In assessing their own behavior, for instance, 54 percent of women in this age group said they were more likely to acquire thirty pairs of shoes than to save $30,000 for retirement, and three-fourths have outstanding debt, with typical credit card balances between $2,000 and $3,000.[2] If this mismatch extends further, the consequences of real life may be lost in the *Myst*. The kid who masters a 360 in a Tony Hawk skateboarding game weathers plenty of crashes. She thinks she's robust—but she might not be prepared for executing real skateboard tricks, where the crashes hurt. Business, too, includes real pain. You can lose everything, or face the burden of laying off people who counted on you. Even back when "serial entrepreneur" was a compliment, those early bankruptcies only sounded romantic. The lucky few who got to be young dot-com execs knew all that, but did they *really* know, until it happened? By now, they might have learned a valuable lesson about real pain; but what about the millions of future leaders in their peer group? Will *their* pattern of taking risks, learned "in there," work out here? How will they respond to real failure?

Trial and Error

We'll know soon, because members of the game generation embrace risk even more often than they realize. That's because they know, from countless attempts to maneuver through fictional mazes and dungeons, that trial and error is the preferred way to tackle any problem. There's no time to read boring manuals or take a course on Advanced Dungeon Navigation Strategies. And honestly, why would you bother? Even if those methods are a little more efficient, they are a lot less fun. Of course, as scholars such as Obe Hostetter have pointed out, this approach—being forced to "learn the rules through trial and error, observation, and hypothesis testing"—is the essence of inductive discovery.[3] Games provide countless opportunities to test and retest different problem-solving strategies immediately and without heavy preparation. (Who ever heard of warming up to play video games?) Marc Prensky said it best:

> "RTFM" ("read the [expletive] manual") is a term of derision. They'll just play with the software, hitting every key if necessary, until they figure it out. If they can't, they assume the problem is with the software, not with them. This attitude is almost certainly a direct result of growing up with Sega, Nintendo, and other video games where each level and monster had to be figured out by

trial and error, and each trial click might lead to a hidden surprise or "Easter egg."[4]

Here we confront another part of the generation gap. For boomers, trial and error was never something to be proud of. Think of the Ron Howard film, *Apollo 13*, in which a crippled American spacecraft drifted toward the moon. The ship had to be returned to Earth using only its remaining fuel and supplies. One key problem, finding a start-up sequence that would use much less power than normal, was handled by trial and error using a simulator back in Houston. But setting the target for that task—and just about every other step involved—depended on serious mental work: engineers working furiously on slide rules, filling blackboards with calculations, all focused on arriving at trustworthy solutions *in advance*. Failure was famously "not an option"; neither, in contrast to video game rules, was just trying stuff out. Howard's film captured the spirit of those times. Right in the middle of the baby boom's coming of age, the space mission approach was taken as the gold standard, not just at NASA but in academic work at all levels and in professionally run businesses and well-advised public sector organizations. Trial and error would have seemed unsophisticated, inefficient, and, well, slightly embarrassing.

Gamers can barely imagine such an attitude. For them, trial and error is not only a legitimate tool; it's their standard. Manuals *are* ignored. "Training missions" are just structured trial and error. The way you learn to use the grenades in *Metal Gear Solid* or to build a stable nation-state in *Civilization* is by doing it. Players like it that way. After all, training missions could be mandatory, with a strong dose of reading and lecture, perhaps like your company's training programs. But reviewers and players would hate that. (Your employees don't mind at all—right?)

Of course, trial and error has some advantages. In the digital world, you're only wasting electrons, so experimentation *is* cheap. Doing *is* more fun than studying. Experience *is* a powerful teacher. (Just the other day, a ten-year-old explained a recent game to us, "My first civilization collapsed, because I only included one city in it. When I refused to pay the bad guys, they attacked that city, and my whole civilization fell apart." Which will stick longer—that memory or a lecture on diversifying a portfolio?) Sometimes, trial and error is even the best analytic route; we might know the equations for everything, but filling in the constants, variables, and limits can be impossible. With the Internet, sophisticated customer databases, and other technologies, it might be more effective to simply test pricing or feature sets rather than make serious estimates in advance.

What the power of trial and error forces us to admit is at the very core of this new generation gap. It helps us to understand the game generation's attitudes toward risk and even to decide where those attitudes might be useful. But it goes much further. It's the central secret of digital gaming, maybe even secret from gamers themselves: *Games are providing real, valuable experience.* True, gaming experience is not the same experience you get from actually working. It certainly doesn't model any part of the real world all that consistently. And it is often outrageous in tone. But it does offer real experience solving problems that, however fantastic their veneers, seem real to the player. When gamers head off to play, they are escaping. But as we saw earlier, they end up in an odd-looking educational environment. (Take a look, for example, at the world of Neopets, outlined in box 6-1.) What they learn there sticks. And at least some of it really counts. As we've seen, it changes their attitudes. It also gives them

BOX 6-1: HOW MUCH IS THAT DOGGY IN THE WINDOWS?

Neopets is one of the most popular kids' sites on the Web—most of its nearly sixty million members spend hours there. And it's making money; launched in April 2000, it became profitable a few months later, and has been ever since. Neopets refuses to disclose earnings, but at one point it had projected $12 million to $15 million in revenues for 2002. It's also a fine example of the challenging fictional worlds that gamers take for granted—places where "playing" really means "solving problems." Take a look at what Neopet members, most younger than eighteen, must do:

- **Design Good Pets**. This choice is important; virtual happiness and prosperity are at stake. It is also surprisingly complex. Players get to choose everything from species, gender, and color to how their new friend reacts to strangers (for example, "smile sweetly," "insult from a distance," and so on). So far, it sounds as if the only trick is choosing wisely, which is still not all that easy. But vital traits like strength are determined by a random number generator; you have five tries to get a desirable combination of characteristics. On the fifth roll of the dice, you have to live with the results.
- **Maintain Them Forever**. You can improve your pet by reading to it, playing with it, or taking it to the hospital for a checkup. You must take care of it; otherwise, it becomes surly, catches a cold, or becomes very, very sad. But unlike Tamagotchi, these pets can't die. You're stuck with them. You can give them to the pound, but even

then you have to pay the emotional price (clicking buttons repeatedly while the pet begs you not to) and pay financially for their upkeep while they are there. In virtual terms, this is serious, if not lifelong, responsibility—sort of like hiring a new direct report.

- **Compete with Others**. Battle, of course, is a mainstay. You can challenge any other pet on the system to a battle. The best moves can be seen in instant replay. But there are also beauty contests in which players get to pit the pets they have designed (or customized; we can tell you from experience that young players can spend *hours* customizing their pets with paintbrushes they find in their game travels). Both battle and beauty contests can earn Neopoints, but pride is at least as important as a reward.
- **Make Money**. Players can make money through work, business, or investment. As in the real world, life in the world of Neopia takes cash (thinly disguised as Neopoints). You can get it through work or through trade (auctioning off items that you've found as you wander around Neopia) using a system much like eBay. There's also investment: in the Neodaq stock market, the safe but low-return National Neopian Bank, and, for the truly adventurous, a commodities broker named Nigel.
- **Community Service**. Beyond cash and prizes, Neopia even makes room for altruism. Members have been asked to help fend off common threats, such as a Tyrannian invasion. In that case, company executives were surprised at the response: some twenty thousand pets arrived to join the defense. That's twenty thousand volunteers in just five hours, an effort executives had expected would take an entire weekend.

experience with fairly realistic problems. Gamers are like seasoned travelers or professionals with years of experience. They have seen a wide range of characters and environments; faced hundreds of dramatic challenges in a safe, resilient, ultimately logical setting; and experienced more incidents of failure and success in just a year or two than most of us have in a lifetime.

Gaming experience can also be surprisingly complex, and surprisingly applicable to business life. A typical example is from Neopets: Like many games, this one sprinkles the virtual world with items that players can find and collect. As we write this, Neopets is the second most popular site on the Web, according to Alexa (a Web service that lets you see how many hits a site gets). Some sixty million people, 80 percent of them younger than eighteen, have signed up for this cross between a game and a portal.[5] As Neopet owners, they adopt electronic pets, nurture them, challenge other pet owners to fight, buy and sell goods, and even play the Neodaq stock market to accumulate more Neopoints (which help their pets live happier, more fulfilled lives). Neopet players value these fictional pets enough to pay real money for them—so much so that there are attempts to trade Neopet accounts on eBay (attempts that eBay does its best to suppress, but supply and demand are nonetheless there). In an extreme case, one British boy went straight to the source, offering the Neopets company itself £100 (about $180) for one billion Neopoints.

Two high school–aged sisters we observed tracked their results on the Neopets site. They couldn't see any significant difference in the items they found. (Since the items are randomly generated, that would make sense. If each collects a reasonable number of items, their average value should be comparable.) But one sister grew very rich from these auctions;

the other made almost nothing. That's three lessons, at least: Life isn't fair; in a free market, value is set by what buyers are willing to pay; and it's easy to go broke guessing the taste of teenagers, even if you are one. The first two, at least, sound pretty basic. But how many college graduates, taking their first business jobs, really understand those principles in an intuitive way? And how many executives, of whatever age, could have used just one more lesson on the third? Now imagine what it's like to learn these market realities the hard way before you're old enough to drive.

The game generation, at least, clearly believes that they have learned from this kind of experience. As one young manager pointed out, "I'm into a lot of strategy games; they help you think more logically." Another saw similar benefits from a different genre: "In role-playing games like *Zelda* you face decisions; you have to make choices, learn in the early stages the consequences of some actions. You choose to do one thing, your player dies. It teaches the consequences of risk and encourages analytical thinking and planning through experience." Gamers' belief in their own skills goes beyond other people's money, too. We also see members of the game generation moving more confidently, and in some ways more capably, into complex areas such as finance. Half of Americans aged sixteen to twenty-two, for example, save a portion of their money; nearly 11 percent invest in mutual funds; and as many own stock.[6] That level of financial activity and awareness was not happening back in the 1970s, when boomers were about this age.

So gamers understand risk/reward. The game world has given them experience with it, in many contexts with many, *many* trials; and that experience is even somewhat realistic. Gamers themselves believe that they have learned professional skills from their gaming experiences. But do their risk-taking attitudes really translate into significant business potential? Can such attitudes really be useful? As the data in the next chapter demonstrates, the answer is clearly yes: Partly through their thinking about risk, and partly through other lessons, video games have produced a generation of potential executives.

CHAPTER SEVEN

Gamers on Top

WHAT TO EXPECT FROM GAMERS AS EXECUTIVES

At this point, it's easy to imagine a hypothetical boomer staring into the future and seeing only an abyss. No, not *that* abyss—one a little less personal, but almost as scary. Gamers, he would see, can be great professionals or even great team players. But at some point, whether the rest of us like it or not, they will also become CEOs and other senior executives, leading the economy throughout our retirement. Even if all your own money were in bonds, *that* thought could inspire real dread. "After all," our boomer might say, "we've already seen these kids crash and burn the sector they invented—and take our 401(k) money with them. If the dot-com meltdown was bad, imagine what they can do with a whole economy."

Our data suggests the opposite: Members of the game generation have the makings of great CEOs.

Leaders? We Don't Need No Stinking Leaders!

The idea that gamers could be great CEOs sounds unlikely. Our own first impression was that gamers would make *exciting* CEOs—but not ones we'd trust with our own retirement funds. For starters, *in the world in which gamers grow up, leaders are basically useless.* It's not that there is no hierarchy at all. It's just that the hierarchy, especially the part above you, is irrelevant or evil.

Rebellion is gaming's classic theme. Racing games feature outrunning the highway patrol. A snowboarding game like *Dark Summit* might send you on a mission to break down "no snowboarding" signs or to deliberately knock down the ski patrol. Then there's the *Hit Man* series and *Grand Theft Auto*, in which "you can pick up a prostitute, pay her for (offscreen) services, then kill her and get your money back."[1] In real (gaming) life, too, players—like their characters—have no use for authority. There are no coaches; what instruction exists is light, voluntary, and concealed with attitude (*Spiderman*), charisma (*Tomb Raider*), or the pure kinetic fun of driving fast machines and blowing stuff up (*Star Wars: Rogue Leader*). Why the camouflage? The game generation believes in skill; they don't believe in following orders. On all the dimensions they care about, the game generation is on its own.

This emphasis on self-reliance characterizes not only how they think, but also what they do. We hear complaints from midlevel managers (typically boomers) that their new employees (typically gamers) seem to solve problems by successive approximation: "I'm having to review work product from my team three and four times—it's as if making the Power-Point is so easy, they just throw something together that looks good but hasn't really been thought through. And they think

that's normal—they try something out on me, I find the problems, they fix that, I find more. Repeat until deadline. They
don't understand that by the time I see something, it ought to
be as right as they can make it." That *does* have a careless
sound, doesn't it?

Careless, disrespectful, sheltered from the real costs of
their mistakes—are these the people we want running the
economy when we're finally ready to get serious about golf?
In a word, yes. Because *gamers are natural-born executives.*
While they were experimenting heedlessly in that sheltered,
leaderless environment, they learned a few things. And those
subconscious lessons are perfect for rising business leaders.
When you look at the data, you find that game experience has
encouraged three traits that are crucial for executives:

- As we saw in the last chapter, gamers take risks—but
  only for the right reasons.
- Gamers "think different"—they fit easily into flexible organizations.
- Gamers "go meta"—they have a leader's perspective on
  success, failure, and perspective itself.

Gamers "Think Different"

There's no denying that gamer executives will be different
from their predecessors. That difference is exactly what will
make them great CEOs. The organizations they will run are
already much different from the ones boomers grew up in.
We all know that; a decade or two of experience has shown
us all that the traditional model no longer really works. Our
corporations have had to become less rigid, more global, and

a lot better at responding on the fly. They have made that transition, for the most part, and so have we. In a stagnant growth economy, companies are being hollowed out; employees who remain behind work harder, but they also have to work smarter and differently. We've come to take such changes for granted, but there's always that step of translating from the old model to the new.

It's natural that boomer executives would need that translation. No matter how smart or adaptable, they did not grow up in a world of constant change and complicated matrix structures. Back then, CEOs might have thought about stakeholders, but they sure didn't talk about them. A "network" was one-to-many transmission with no return path—like traditional TV. And the businesspeople who created the largest "brick-and-mortar" corporations drew their ideas from a simple source: the military, with its rectilinear organization charts and simple chain of command. Originally, that theoretical simplicity was tempered by messy experience. Many executives had been on real battlefields. They knew that nothing really went as expected; as a retired colonel once told us, with the air of vast repetition, "It's not the plan, it's the planning." And they knew what really high stakes were. As the baby boom proceeded, the military model remained, but was more often experienced at one remove. The thinking began to come from combat-oriented sports, rather than the battlefield itself. Strategy got defined as something between a war game map and a Vince Lombardi diagram of the playing field in which you could keep track of competitors and customers in one glance; nothing better than a good chalk talk over a two-by-two matrix. Of course, team sports aren't much like real warfare, but they do convey some of the same experience-based lessons. You *have* to play with other people; you can only play a certain number of times; timing isn't under your control; and "taking a hit" or "having skin in the game" really hurts. Commands come from above. Almost equally vital, because communication is cumbersome, strategy is set once, changed only with deliberation, and is generally the province of bosses alone. Other people in the organization are actually told things like "we're not paying you to think."

Boomers still in business have long since changed from that model to something a little more flexible. But gamers, as we have seen, were already there—and maybe far beyond. Video games aren't just one more remove away from combat; they're a different beast entirely. Individual control, trial and error, and constant change are all just part of life. We believe that this experience, and the mental models that came with it, made the dot-coms possible. Certainly the new rules of corporate life—the ones we boomers have been talking ourselves into for years now—seem perfectly obvious to people who grew up with digital games.

Gamers Are Naturally Global

Part of what gamers understand, automatically, is the lack of simple structure—the kind of change globalization has made necessary. If you're doing complicated tasks in a fast-changing environment, the chain of command tends to get a little messy. Another part of organizational life they take for granted is globalization itself. We boomers might work for transnational corporations but—take it from someone who has trained and consulted with hundreds of senior executives valiantly attempting to "go global"—the old home-office mentality is alive and well just about everywhere. Again, it goes back to the way we grew up in business. The corporate world that boomers first learned about had a powerful headquarters in the country of origin. That was the center of a literal empire; the job of the provinces was to do corporate's bidding and send back plenty of tribute. This nationalistic focus wasn't just internal. The home market was the real one; everything else was literally subsidiary. That perspective doesn't make economic sense any more, so we tell ourselves to somehow lose these attitudes lodged deep in our bones. Some of us even succeed. Gamers needn't even try. Those old models would never even occur to them. The game generation is deeply, truly global. Don't ask how they'd do on a geography test. Give a cross-section of American business professionals an unlabeled map and ask them to fill in rivers and capitals, and our money would be on the oldest respondents. But ask them to draw a conceptual map of the business world and there's one key thing that the gamers would certainly get right: The United States won't be alone at the center. Why would it? Any serious gamer knows the best games are from Japan. So are most of the cool platforms and devices—not to mention an awful lot of serious players.

Gamers are a global generation to begin with. World music is a form of pop to them, not a strange new section at Tower. *Anime* is more familiar than *Archie*. Games have supercharged globalization because they are so easily ported over. The story lines are simple and universal, even formulaic. Localization is easy. And gamers are definitely a global market. By global standards, they have to be fairly affluent, but millions are found in just about every major market. It's even possible that, worldwide, these people have more in common with each other than with people who share their nationality, history, and educational background, but not their experience with games.

Gamers Pace Themselves

The final aspect of "thinking different"—of gamers' natural ability to lead the nontraditional corporation—is simple: They don't learn like we do. In an economy that prizes self-service of all kinds, the game generation delivers something even better: It is self-educating.

This drive is the flip side of a potential weakness we saw earlier. Gaming has created an entirely different learning style, one that:

- Aggressively ignores any hint of formal instruction
- Leans heavily on trial and error (after all, failure is nearly free; you just push "play again")
- Includes lots of learning from peers but virtually none from authority figures
- Is consumed in very small bits exactly when the learner wants, which is usually just before the skill is needed.

As one midcareer professional put it, "Trial-and-error learning a lot of times works best for me. Sometimes it can take a little longer to figure things out for myself, but once I screw something up, I can be sure I'm not going to do that one again. I definitely prefer a hands-on component." Other respondents have said, "If you give me a short booklet and it's not complicated, OK, but the best way for me to learn is hands-on: doing it, doing it again and doing it again, then getting it"; or "Training would be much more effective if it was more interactive, like a game, with input and interaction with the system. I don't mind whether it's a computer or a person, it just has to be more interactive than just reading."

The relatively young gamers who made these comments expect far more radical change in their even younger counterparts. Many people in our survey noted that early exposure to sophisticated games had obvious results. "It's scary what six- and seven-year-olds can do on a PC," said one. "My eight-year-old nephew blows me away on *Crash Bandicoot*," said another. "My nephew is four. He plays PlayStation games because his father loves them. These games seem much more strategy oriented, less arcade-style." During the baby boom, kindergarten teachers looked for children to show up knowing, say, the names of their colors; in this generation, they show up as budding strategists. That difference might not be clear to pre–game-generation teachers, but it's true, just the same.

A Relentless Drive to Make Things Better

Experience has prepared gamers for twenty-first-century business; they learn on the fly, think globally, and don't count on fixed organizational structures. So in the ways that tomorrow's CEOs will need to, they "think different." But that experience has also given this group something vital for top executives in any age: a sustained, early chance to develop the leader's perspective.

The innovators at Xerox Palo Alto Research Center (PARC)—one of the most creative R&D institutions ever, though famously not a financial prize—used to say that "point of view is worth fifty IQ points." They probably weren't talking about organizational aptitude, but they might as well have been. To succeed, leaders must have the right perspective, including the ability to change perspective as needed. Without it, they simply can't identify the critical choices, much less make them. Nor can they survive the potentially shattering experience of choosing wrong, or even choosing right and facing the consequences.

That perspective begins with productive dissatisfaction. Leaders, at least in business, are supposed to drive you forward. For that, you need a goal—a sense that things could be better. Gaming experience produces that sense. We saw earlier that gamers care about their organizations, but are willing to pull the plug if they can't achieve what they want. That trait goes beyond their feelings about the company. *The more time you have spent playing games, the more you believe that things can be made better.* Presented with the statement, "My life could be happier than it is now," nearly 70 percent of frequent gamers from this generation agree (see figure 7-1). That number is clearly more than their less experienced agemates. And in both generations, the more gaming experience you have, the more you agree with this statement. It's important to understand that this survey item does not measure unhappiness, depression, or dissatisfaction with life in general.

FIGURE 7-1

My Life Could Be Happier Than It Is Now

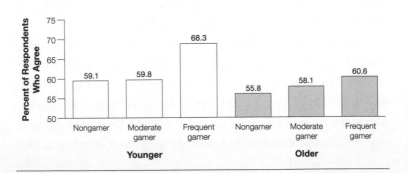

Instead, it reflects what might be summarized as ambition or internal drive: the ability to imagine a more desirable state, and to believe that reaching this state is possible. That tendency, so strong in gamers, might not make you happier day-to-day than others; but it certainly makes for more driven executives.

Gamers Get Tough

This attitude matches perfectly with the experience of gaming. Strangely, it's not always fun in there. Frustration, disappointment, and believing that a particular game is unbeatable are all par for the course. At least one of the authors has himself been tempted to hurl game controllers across the room as (purely in the interest of science) he found himself stuck for the fifth time in the depths of some Mayan tomb, fending off vampire bats and hungry wolves, with no treasure in sight— nowhere to go at all, really. And the evidence strongly suggests that, at moments like these, simply knowing on the rational level that there must be some answer doesn't fend off frustration. We don't believe the game generation is immune to this experience; among the heavy gamers we know, there often seems to be a title on the shelf that never gets played simply because it's too hard (or, which is simultaneously true and easier for a gamer to admit, "not that much fun").

But the reality is that, despite the frustrations of an individual session, you do always *know* that there's an answer. There will turn out to be a secret door actuated by twisting the light fixture, or an extra-high jump command, or a way to shoot the wolves from above so they won't be nipping at your feet while the vampire bats are circling your head. A newly minted M.B.A., looking back on simpler (virtual) times, put it this way: *"Super Mario Bros.* was a puzzle, a maze, and a trial, but there was a clear end goal—save the princess—and everyone knew you could somehow reach it. The game would have lost all meaning without it." In the game world, it is always simply a matter of using the resources you have: patience (once you have taken a break); innovative thinking (game problems seem just as likely to stir up the familiar flash of insight in the shower as "real" problems); brute force (in the game world, if you make your inglorious way down the mountain enough, eventually you will learn to snowboard); help from others (friends, strategy guides, Internet sites, occasionally parents); even reading the hints and instructions provided within the game (many of which pop up just about when you need them). You can be as creative as you want; no solution is unthinkable, because there is always the "new game" button to bail you out, and no real-world consequences. (The necessary and well-intended lies we tell ourselves and our children, say, in the pediatrician's office—"this will only hurt for a minute"—are literally and completely true in the world of digital games. Standards like *Mortal Kombat* and *Street Fighter* let players fight hand-to-hand battles to the death over and over again without a hint of real blood ever being spilled (except perhaps over whose turn it is next). So, in the unique experience of the game generation, *the only real limiting factor, always, is your own willingness to keep trying. The only real driver is your own desire to reach some better state.*

Those attitudes are fine foundations for any leader. But they are not enough. To make good decisions, executives need access to another perspective: the detachment to make the hard decisions.

Getting Some Distance

Fortunately for all of us, playing games—as unlikely as it seems—teaches that detachment, too. We're not saying that video games make you tough or callous. They might, but those aren't exactly the traits leaders need. Yet it's undeniable that, along with ambition, leadership does require a certain distance. CEOs need some insulation from the fear that naturally goes along with risk. If you're obsessed with imagining the costs of failure, it's hard to move boldly toward success. If you can't stop thinking about the damage done by your last mistake, it's tough to avoid the next one. We all want leaders who recognize the full price of mistakes, past and present, for themselves and others, but who can also put that recognition aside when it is no longer useful. This quality doesn't always sound attractive. Certainly it can go too far. But that kind of distance is necessary, and far better for everyone than its opposite.

You can see this distance indirectly in the game generation's attitudes. Some of the survey answers that can make this group sound a little callous, a little like they see everything and everyone as a game—don't they seem just a little more valuable when we think of the ideal leader's perspective? Certainly that's true for many of the learning experiences that the game generation has grown up with. Neopets, for example, puts children in the position of managing their pets. We mean that literally, and we don't just mean providing direction and resources. We mean making the tough decisions with respect to a bunch of cuddly little animals. Each Neopets player has to make the equivalent of real hiring decisions; as in real life, they know what traits they want, but must choose from an imperfect and unpredictable selection presented by the process. With only a few chances at each "hire," they might sometimes reject a workable candidate, hoping for something much better, only to be given candidates who are much worse. Neopet players have to make tough calls at the other end of the pipeline, too. They can get rid of a pet that no longer meets their needs. But—the parallels will be obvious—termination has its costs. Remember, unwanted pets won't just fade away. Ignore them, and they get more and more miserable. Send them to the pound, and you'll have to face, repeatedly and with rising intensity, their plaintive cries for one more chance. Give in, of course, and you're back where you started, stuck with their shortcomings.

If there's a better system for teaching a leader's detachment to preteens without hurting any sentient being, we don't know what it is. But that distance, and, equally important, the ability to choose the right distance for this situation in the game, is built into games much more broadly. As intense and interactive as they are, games automatically teach two things about perspective: first, that a little distance is not just useful, but normal; and second, that your point of view is a choice— and choosing correctly matters.

Gamers Go Meta

These lessons are even taught through literal perspective: whose point of view the game screen presents. Point of view varies by type; first-person-shooters tend toward a first-person view, where the screen shows what your character would be seeing. Many sports titles default to the perspective of a well-produced TV broadcast. But in general, the standard perspective provides a little distance. You feel like you're playing the game—yet not completely lost in it. Some of that feeling comes from an obvious technical limitation: with no holo-decks available yet, you are always watching a screen, listening to speakers, and manipulating a controller. So your mind, even your heart, can be in the game, but your body can't completely forget that you're really in your family room. This distance is also a design decision, one reinforced by the player's own choice. For many games, the preferred view is over your own shoulder. Think about what that means for experience. What would it feel like, in real life, to watch yourself from behind and slightly above? A little distant, a little more analytical? The game also reminds you, by giving you the structured choice of what perspective to take, that the perspective is often under your control. You can switch to watching from overhead, or looking behind, or perhaps even to a first-person perspective. At certain points, choosing the right view can make a big difference; just like executives, with the right set of information, properly arrayed, players make better decisions.

And just like executives, players learn from the built-in distance and the explicit ability to change point of view that "going meta" can be a lifesaver. How many of us believe that, dropped into a real-world paintball game, we would analyze our situation as coolly and react with as much calm as we do when controlling Solid Snake or 007 up there on the screen? One difference, of course, is the stakes. A paintball hit smarts, and there's at least one live player to share our humiliation in real time. Still, paintball, too, is just a game. The much bigger difference is in perspective. For the time you're playing it, the paintball game *is* your reality. It's not actual combat, but it is your whole world. With the digital version, it feels real, sort of, and can be surprisingly engaging. Still, you can fade in and out, and you know that. You have less to be afraid of, you never really forget there's a larger world you can go back to, and you can change your perspective at will.

What that experience teaches you is this: *With distance and control added to your point of view, you achieve more.* You can see the strategic situation faster. You can take bigger risks. You can easily separate the emotions that go with getting hit from the analysis of how to survive the next time. You learn how and why to "go meta"—taking that step back from the immediate situation, analyzing the choices and the odds, and finding the right strategy. And the power of going meta comes through over and over, not just within a game, but as you shift from game to game. By sampling so many different realities, gamers become good at separating the underlying principles from the visible surface. They become analytical and strategic. In a way very parallel to executive experience, perspective begins adding those virtual IQ points the PARC guys were talking about.

Managing Up—Way, Way Up

Clearly, professionals from the game generation have a lot of potential for leadership. The key word, of course, is potential; their comfort with flexible organization, their natural leader's perspective, and their rational embrace of risk won't automatically convert into performance. The challenge is somehow converting all that potential, as yet untapped, into the CEO that your firm needs—not to mention a whole generation of leaders up and down the organization. Does that sound like a lot of effort to invest in a bunch of kids who just haven't bothered to learn the rules all of us know? Maybe.

But it's necessary. You might as well make the best of it. As a hidden bonus—there's always one of those in computer games—reaching out for that leadership potential could drive the kind of leap we saw in the best of the dot-coms. In that era, we know that game-generation thinking produced some major errors in judgment. But we also saw those attitudes produce incredibly flexible, capable, fast-learning young executives. The trick is leveraging their game-enhanced capabilities, correcting for their game-derived blind spots, and helping them learn the difference. That will require change in them, and in the organization. There are at least two steps you can take now to drive those changes in areas where it will help you:

To find the leaders you need, cross the generation gap. Remember (how could you forget?) good leaders are scarce. Our data suggests there may be more of them in this generation than most. But it also shows that they won't be obvious to many of us pregamers, probably including the people who select the future leaders of your company. And these candidates do tend to have some rough edges, especially by boomer standards. So finding the right people, grooming them, and connecting them to the predecessors who will need to promote and mentor them will take some work. One of the most promising tools for crossing the generation gap on a personal level like this is to provide shared experience, almost an apprenticeship path. You need projects where future leaders from the game generation work side by side with current leaders, who are still mainly from the baby boom. Ideally, gamers will learn that real leadership is far more complex than any MMPORPG. And executives will learn to see through the cultural veneer that could easily divide them.

Another way to cross the generation gap for leaders—and we say this in all seriousness—is to *give Game Boys to your board.* (All right, if they are particularly shy or straitlaced, make it an N-Gage or PSP-type game player with a phone or PDA built in. But make sure they know how to play the games.) If they're ever going to understand the customers, staff, and executives rising inexorably through the ranks, they need to feel for themselves the addictive power of certain games, the independence and satisfaction of taking a five-minute *Tetris* break, and the practical problem-solving challenges that lurk just beneath the edgy surface of many games.

Supercharge the proven power of war games. Along with its potential for leadership, the game generation poses some real challenges. To become the great executives they can be, they'll need experiences that:

- Persuade them, after all those hours of being cowboys, that organizations and leaders are a good thing
- Help them see when trial and error is appropriate and when it isn't, and convince their elders that sometimes it is really the best way
- Help them learn the content, context, and culture of the organization. Leadership is about making choices, which depend on knowing the game, the players, and the arena.

That's a set of complex demands. We suspect it is no more complex than a similar list produced for the baby boomers as they were entering business. We know it's different; as we have seen, the two groups grew up in very different places and inherited very different worlds. And we believe all the items on this list, as well as a lot of professional bonding between the generations, can be delivered through a single mechanism: war games.

A gamers' game. Of course, war games, or the tackling of crises in business through simulation, already take place in many large organizations, including some that are quite conservative about executive development strategies. But their value depends on designing and deploying them well and keeping them updated. The U.S. military, which has a number of established technologies, has long invested in networked high-performance simulators, for instance, to capture the gains of technology and bring new power to war games.

Hold the technology. Ironically, for the game generation, war game technology probably doesn't matter. Our experience using simulations in teaching and executive development has been that, especially at higher levels, you might not need a computer at all. You can just play a free-form war game to make things work. Sure, a computer can be useful in the background to keep track of a variety of different variables. But in a game at the top, it is the thinking, the interaction, and the challenge that makes a game work so well. For the game generation, the whole point is to provide a shared experience with the right content set, to demonstrate the real risks facing nonvirtual organizations without actually paying the cost, and to help two very different groups learn to work with one another.

Content is king. Those goals mean that your war games should be designed with a strong group emphasis. They should also be as realistic and uncontrolled in content as possible. The point isn't to hammer in some by-the-book solution, but to let the group deal with problems that weren't anticipated. That's how they'll learn their own limits—and each other's value. You might even look back in company or industry history for cases in which unanticipated problems threw some executive team for a loop.

Not just an off-site. Beyond content, war games for this generation should also be different. For one thing, they don't have to be such a big deal. In fact, they probably shouldn't be. There's no need to reserve this powerful tool for the yearly off-site meeting. In one company in which we introduced war gaming, after a few months a number of groups ran their weekly staff meetings as war games. People didn't present what they were doing each week. Instead, each person would present a challenge they were facing, the group leader would assign others in the room to play the "obstacles" and stakeholders involved in dealing with this problem, and they'd war-game it out. Staff meetings took longer, but they were unbelievably productive—and everyone wanted to attend. (When was the last time *you* looked forward to a staff meeting? How about your staff?) In a generation of corporate leaders that grew up playing complex games, introducing routine war games would be much easier. There will still be the full-out war game off-sites—special scenarios developed, experts brought in, formal red and blue teams, all that. But these rising leaders are *gamers,* after all; give them a chance to play.

War games for the rest of us. Of course, there are few gamer CEOs yet; these people are mainly concentrated at the bottom of your company's org chart. And part of the challenge is to identify the future leaders among them; they will probably look much different than your current leaders did at that age. Extending war game–like activities to lower levels is a great way to identify leadership potential. (The one caveat is to focus such games on the kind of function players already understand. We have found that, when lower-level executives are asked to put themselves into roles such as CEO, the game doesn't work well. Lower-level executives can eventually broaden their perspective to CEO heights, but not usually in a single game.) Integrating war games and other simulations into the middle manager ranks and below is a no-lose proposition. At worst, it will give young managers already trained in the art of gaming a chance to practice their managerial moves. More likely, it will inspire creative group work; we have often seen "gaming mind" take over when participants are taken out of business situations and allowed to play a game. This is one of the places where the next generation of leaders will appear.

CHAPTER EIGHT

Press Start to Continue

WHAT'S NEXT FOR GAMERS—AND US?

THOUGH THEY SEEM an unlikely path to greatness, video games have created a generation with much more potential than your average baby boomer might imagine or even acknowledge. But as high as gamers' potential is to be great professionals, great team players, and even great executives, the change is just beginning to unfold. Anything involving tens of millions of people making use of ever more powerful learning technology, radical new beliefs about at least one branch of reality, and visible changes in such concrete attitudes as when to take a risk and how to treat other people will have a major impact. The lasting effects will no doubt become clear eventually. Whatever change we can see now is probably just the tip of . . . well, you know the rest.

Don't get us wrong: We don't pick that metaphor to say this generation will sink society like a certain ill-fated North Atlantic steamer. But therein lie two lessons: First, even if all you can see is the tip, it at least tells you where to look. And once you know you're in iceberg territory, it would be nice to know as much about icebergs as you can. While it's too early to map out this one in detail, we can get some idea of what such icebergs generally look like, and what this one might mean for your particular business. To do that, watch games and gamers, but think less about them and more about major cultural shifts. After all, that kind of shift is what the game generation is busy creating. Right now, of course, it feels like a generation gap. On one side, we have the boomers, who tend to say things like, "With all those images that flicker and flash, how will they be able to sit down and work with something that takes time to understand?" Or to describe a particular title as "a game that can literally train soldiers to kill."[1] Boomers worry that gamers "won't see any consequences" to actions that, in real life, indeed have dire consequences.[2] Some even conclude that "computer gaming is a massive waste of time, potential, and money because it turns young people into passive vegetables."[3]

On the other side are the gamers, who dismiss fears of violence driven by games as silly; as one said, "I've played *Pac-Man* all my life, and I don't feel the need to eat little balls and listen to disco music."[4] More surprisingly, they can speak eloquently about the great value in their world, which, they fear, the rest of us simply don't see. As another gamer stated, "Games give us freedom to be, think, do, create, destroy. They let us change the answer to the question 'who am I?' in ways never before possible. Games let us reach the highest highs and lowest lows, let us play with reality and reshape it to our own ends. They give us hope and meaning, show us that our journey through life is not pointless, and help us accomplish something at the end of the day."

Would you have expected such significance from video games? Neither would we. In fact, try as we might, we simply cannot imagine finding meaning in life through a video game. That inability to even imagine a younger group's point of view is a pretty good definition of a generation gap. And thinking of this as a new generation gap begins to tell us what to expect. Like all generation gaps, this one won't stay around all that long. Remember *the* generation gap—or at least the first to bear the name? Sure, we do, too. But when is the last time you referred to it, or needed to, except as pure history? That generation gap stopped being relevant a long time ago. We boomers, like today's game generation, had time, numbers, and maybe even progress on our side. So instead of stagnating into persistent generational war, the culture simply changed around us. We remember; it didn't feel all that simple at the time. But before long, boomer attitudes, values, and behaviors were part of the environment. It didn't matter whether you shared them or not, as an individual, or an executive, or even a whole company. It didn't even matter whether they were good or bad. They just were.

That cultural shift had implications for all kinds of business. Look at magazine ads from the 1940s. They sell Coke, say, by appealing to what would be seen today as saccharine family values. Then came the baby boom; by 1962, cola makers had to appeal, literally, to the "Pepsi generation." Now watch the famous Pepsi commercial from 2001, in which elder statesman Bob Dole essentially cedes his spokesperson status to the arguably overexposed young star, Britney Spears. Could there be a clearer demonstration that the younger generation ultimately wins? Here was a bona fide national leader, a member of the World War II–era "greatest generation," who made real sacrifices in the war—the good war—before the baby boomers were even conceived, being used as the punch line of a joke. The core of the joke was that the powerful emotions that the ad appealed to had nothing to do with family values.

Advertising is far from the only part of business that feels the impact of shifts like this one. Ultimately, just about everything follows culture. Look at corporate structure. The boomers' fathers or mothers were thrilled to be "organization people." Boomers themselves wanted something glitzier, more focused on the individual, with more upside. That desire brought us the go-go environment of the 1980s and 1990s; mobility was in, security was out. The dot-com era, fueled of course by gamers, took that focus on the individual to a whole new level. Employees and employers suddenly, implicitly agreed that every employee, every executive, was really just a free agent. That idea might not look as attractive now as it did during the boom—but it seems no less real.

Those changes, and the forces that drive them, are harder to measure than gamers' professional potential. But they are probably just as important. The game generation will not change business by just their business skill, their work ethic, or even their leadership potential. They will change business by who they are as a whole. How they grew up, how they see the world, what they want, even how they rear their own children—all those qualities matter, too. In short, sooner rather than later, it will be the game generation's culture.

The first step in getting a handle on that evolving culture— and a preview of what's next from this generation—is to think about what gamers' lives are like, and how they differ from the models we all carry around in our heads.

Growing Up Gamer

"Culture" sometimes seems like a soft and imprecise concept. But anthropologists commonly use a precise and extremely practical definition: the set of knowledge, beliefs, and assumptions that is *shared and passed on by the group*. Culture isn't everything we know; it's everything we all know together. Some cultures, for instance, "know" that a particular substance (say, pork) is food; others "know" that it's poison. Those bits of cultural knowledge aren't really individual discoveries or decisions; they belong to the group. They persist longer and are more powerful, generally, than any individual member. They help define the group, and can certainly help us predict behavior, whether in humans or orangutans.

Culture is largely instilled, of course, during childhood. That's what socialization is. We've already seen that a gamer's childhood is sharply different from the traditional kind. But think about how profound those differences are. Gamers grow up *playing* differently. They're not as isolated as parents often fear, but they do have the ability to go off alone whenever they want without boredom. They *learn* differently. It might not be the games versus grades trade-off that some of us expect. But their game experience, at least, emphasizes independent problem solving and the rapid acquisition of technical skills, as opposed to sustained attention to the subtleties of Shakespeare or calculus. They *feel* differently, too. The superficial worry is that playing violent games will make them violent. The larger concern, in our view, is that the simple, structured, and generally competitive relationships allowed during video game playing might not give them the room to develop complex interpersonal skills. *Thinking*, too, is different in their world. We haven't found evidence of the much-feared short attention spans. We have seen a remarkable ability to focus on a single complex task for hours or days at a time. *Growing up* is simply different for gamers. They have replaced whatever traditional experiences they might have had as supporting players with a dramatic increase in experiencing the hero role; they've had more experience with repeated failure that builds toward success, but probably less experience with activities where they'll never be the best, or even average.

These experiences fashion a workforce that is full of surprises for the managers around them. Gamers can look like arrogant slackers at first glance, yet turn out to be highly motivated and energetic—with a high need to choose and star in their own "missions." They can seem distant from others, yet they value the team, and the people around them, more than people without game experience. And though they grow up in an environment without many model leaders, they seem skilled at leadership—at taking risks, at managing people, at taking the strategic view. All these things are, in a way, merely the first-order effects. Many of us, in business and in the rest of life, will have to deal with the complexities that follow from the initial differences explored here. And at this point, it's hard to tell where this generation is going.

Getting Inside Their Heads

We can see it's going somewhere, and soon. Long before most of us expect it, we will be surrounded by gamers in various roles—as subordinates, coworkers, and bosses, yes, but also as friends, acquaintances, and loved ones. If you haven't experienced this change already, it's only a matter of time.

So, armed with the information we have about gamers, knowing big changes are coming and are not yet clear, what can we do? Two strategies seem simple, cheap, and worthwhile.

First is the "when in Rome" strategy: To really get inside game culture, you have to at least know the specifics of how gamers prefer to spend their free time. You don't have to become a gamer—we'd recommend you not try. But it does seem wise to get a feel for what is going on. Depending on your circumstances, that might mean actually playing a game or two, or truly watching, really paying attention, to what your children play. It can also mean—in fact it *should*—building a real relationship with a gamer you know professionally. The best bet would be finding one, or recruiting one, into the team around you. Finally, go nuts with some cultural tourism. Hang out in an Electronics Boutique; wrangle an invitation to a LAN party; take a Game Boy on your next road trip. But remember to look past the superficial parts of games and focus on the life lessons they impart.

The second strategy is more "what if?" By doing some very light, game-specific scenario planning, you might be able to find areas that bear watching for your particular business concerns. Beginning with the real and potential changes outlined here, identify the ones that seem most likely to touch on your business. Maybe it's a way to make heroes out of your employees. Maybe it's one of those broad cultural changes we know are coming. For each area, spend half an hour brainstorming what could happen, how it could threaten you, and how you could exploit it. And—most important—identify signposts, indicators that would tell you, early, whether that change is taking place.

A final caveat: Games and gamers are known for nothing if not their exceedingly quick evolution. So it's worth remembering that to really stay on top of this phenomenon, you're going to have to keep up. As more and more stories about video games float to the surface of our culture (easily more than four thousand will be published this year alone), it would behoove you to pay attention to the ins and outs of what gamers are thinking not only today, but also tomorrow. It's going to take some effort on your part, but in the end it will be worth it, because it will lead you to think about, notice, and respond to the right things out of thousands competing for your attention. In other words, it will keep you in the game.

A final note: As the game generation's impact continues, so does our research. We would greatly appreciate hearing your thoughts, experiences, and observations on the topic. Simply e-mail us: data@gotgamebook.com

Behavioral Patterns of the Game Generation

Gaming Experience by Category

Four-fifths of younger survey respondents say they were moderate or frequent gamers as teens, compared with only one-third of older respondents.

FIGURE A-1

Teenage Gaming Experience by Category

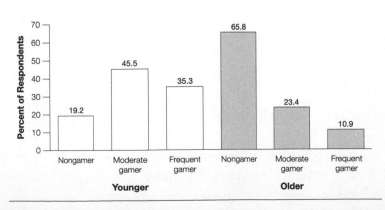

Gamers Want More Out of Life

Gamers play to do the things they can't do in real life.

- Gamers are less likely to think their lives are comfortable and secure (46.6 percent of frequent younger gamers agree versus 57.1 percent of older nongamers).
- Gamers are more likely to do their own thing (82.7 percent of frequent younger gamers agree versus 74 percent of older nongamers).
- Gamers believe the most important thing in life is experiencing all emotions (52.6 percent of frequent younger gamers agree versus 45.3 percent of older nongamers).

FIGURE A-2

I Play to Do the Things I Can't in Real Life

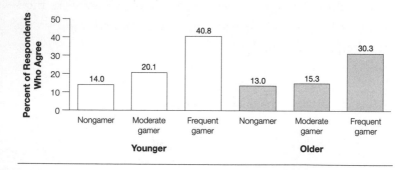

Gamers' Relationship with Money

Gamers believe it is important to receive a high salary and good benefits (75.4 percent of frequent younger gamers agree versus 66.3 percent of younger nongamers).

FIGURE A-3

It Is Important to Receive a High Salary and Good Benefits

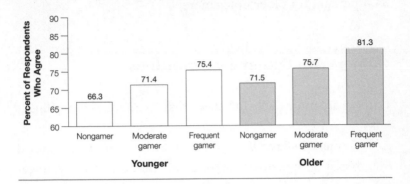

Gamers are more likely to spend a $3,000 bonus on enter-tainment electronics (12 percent of frequent younger gamers agree versus 1.4 percent of younger nongamers and 3.8 per-cent of older nongamers.

Gamers Are More Social

Gamers have a higher need for other human relationships.

FIGURE A-4

Need for Human Relations

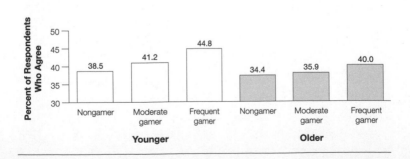

Those who grew up playing games see playing as a social experience (49.5 percent for frequent younger gamers versus 34.4 percent for older nongamers).

Gamers Are Extremely Ambitious

Gamers are more likely to believe that "winning is everything."

- Gamers believe if anything is to be done right, they'd better do it themselves (74.6 percent of frequent younger gamers agree versus 55.5 percent of older nongamers).
- Gamers are more likely to go out of their way to make friends with powerful people (31.9 percent of frequent younger gamers agree versus 18.8 percent of older nongamers).

FIGURE A-5

Winning Is Everything

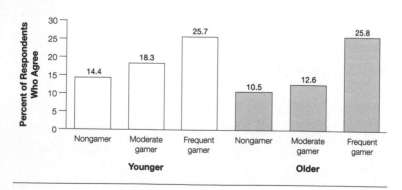

Gamers' View of Their Coworkers

Gamers believe people won't work hard unless they're forced to do so.

- Gamers believe the best way to handle people is to tell them what they want to hear (27.7 percent of frequent younger gamers agree versus 16.5 percent of older non-gamers).
- Gamers believe they can control the way they come across to make the right impression (80.1 percent of frequent younger gamers agree versus 74.1 percent of older nongamers).

FIGURE A-6

People Won't Work Hard Unless They're Forced to Do So

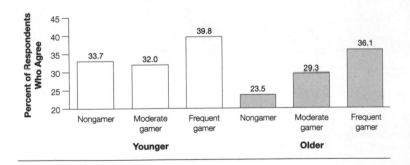

Notes

Acknowledgments

1. For those interested in research methods, subjects for our qualitative interviews were a diverse population, though not a random one. Those whose quotes throughout the book help illustrate the patterns found in our statistical work, were drawn from a wide range of business professionals. These included recent graduates of two MBA programs; employees of large organizations in financial services, management consulting, high technology, manufacturing, health care, and government; and professionals from a variety of smaller companies, including those focused on marketing, retail, and higher education. We and our research colleagues also interviewed a number of people who have just entered the workforce (including students from large universities on the West Coast and in the Midwest), and some who are members of gamers' families or households.

Introduction

1. Interactive Digital Software Association, "2001 Consumer Survey," 17 May 2001, < http://www.idsa.com/consumersurvey2001.html> (accessed 17 December 2003); U.S. Department of Commerce, Bureau of the Census, *Population Projections of the United States by Age, Sex, Race, and Hispanic Origin: 1995 to 2050* (Washington, DC: GPO, 1996).

2. Bureau of the Census, *Population Projections of the United States by Age, Sex, Race, and Hispanic Origin*.

3. National Institute on Media and the Family, "Fact Sheet: Media Use," < http://www.mediafamily.org/facts/facts_mediause.shtml > (accessed 21 January 2004).

4. John Markoff, "Microsoft's Game Plan; Xbox to Go Head to Head with Sony," *New York Times*, 4 September 2000.

5. Jonathan Dee, "Playing Mogul," *New York Times*, 21 December 2003.

6. Stuart Elliott and Bill Carter, "Nielsen Offers More Details on Lost Viewers," *New York Times*, 25 November 2003.

7. Entertainment Software Association, "Top Ten Industry Facts," < http://www.theesa.com/pressroom.html > (accessed 14 January 2004).

8. Kim Miyoung, "South Korea Grapples with Online Gaming Addicts," *Reuters*, 11 January 2004; Thor Olavsrud, "NCsoft, SINA Team to Bring Lineage to China," Internet.com, 22 November 2002, < http://asia.internet.com/news/article.php/1546831 > (accessed May 10, 2004).

9. Hiawatha Bray, "Justice Has Its Price in the Sim World," *Boston Globe*, 14 January 2004.

10. Marcia C. Smith, "Fantasy Becomes Reality," *Orange County Register*, 2 November 2003.

11. IDC, Framingham, MA. "2001 Video Game Survey," 31 August 2001.

12. Euromonitor, "Consumer Expenditure on Leisure and Recreation: Euromonitor from National Statistics," Euromonitor Market Database, 2004, < http://www.euromonitor.com/gmid/ >.

13. "Croft Beats Jolie for Top Billing," *The Dominion [Wellington]*, 15 June 2001.

14. Entertainment Software Association, "Top Ten Industry Facts."

15. Ziff Davis, "Next-Generation Consoles Set to Explode Gaming Industry, Finds Gaming Survey," press release, 7 August 2001.

16. At U.S. Spelling Bee, a Prize for 'Pococurante,'" *New York Times*, 30 May 2003.

17. Omar L. Gallaga, "Up-and-Down Console Game Industry Enjoying Best Popularity Since Days of Atari 2600," *Austin American-Statesman*, 7 October 1998.

18. Paul Trueman, "Old School Games," *The Guardian (London)*, 19 July 2001.
19. Milt Freudenheim, "Drug Spending Rises Sharply at Pharmacies and by Mail," *New York Times*, 29 March 2002.
20. David K. Foot and Daniel Stoffman, *Boom, Bust and Echo 2000: Profiting From the Demographic Shift in the New Millennium* (Toronto: Macfarlane, Walter and Ross, 1998); U.S. Department of Education, National Center for Education Statistics, *Projections of Education Statistics to 2010* (Washington, DC: GPO, 2000); Bureau of the Census, *Population Projections of the United States by Age, Sex, Race, and Hispanic Origin*.
21. Noel C. Paul, "New Video Consoles Not Just for Kids," *Christian Science Monitor (Boston, MA)*, 10 January 2001.

Chapter 1

1. Craig Smith, KGUN, Tuscon, AZ, "Cell Phones and Kids," < http://www.kgun9.com/story.asp?TitleID = 3577&ProgramOption = News > (accessed 21 January 2004).
2. Two starting points we particularly recommend are Rusel Demaria and Johnny L. Wilson, *High Score! The Illustrated History of Electronic Games* (Berkeley, CA: McGraw-Hill/Osborne, 2002) and David Sheff, *Game Over* (Wilton, CT: GamePress, 1999).
3. Sheff, *Game Over*.
4. Susan Moffat, "Can Nintendo Keep Winning?" *Fortune*, 5 November 1990, 131.
5. John Markoff, "From PlayStation to Supercomputer for $50,000," *New York Times*, 26 May 2003.
6. P. M. Greenfield, *Media and the Mind of the Child: From Print to Television, Video Games and Computers* (Cambridge, MA: Harvard University Press, 1984).
7. A. S. Oyen and J. M. Bebok, "The Effects of Computer Games and Lesson Contexts on Children's Mnemonic Strategies," *Journal of Experimental Child Psychology* 62, no. 2 (1996): 173–189.
8. Marc Prensky, *Digital Game-Based Learning* (New York: McGraw-Hill, 2001).
9. National Institute on Media and the Family, "Fact Sheet: Media Use," < http://www.mediafamily.org/facts/facts_mediause.shtml > (accessed 21 January 2004).

10. RESI and Towson University, "eReadiness Maryland: Assessing Our Digital Opportunities," Highlights for Press Announcement, 1 June 2002, < http://www.marylandtedco.org/news/pdfs/Highlights_for_press_announcement.pdf > (accessed 17 December 2003).

11. Interactive Digital Software Association, "2001 Consumer Survey," 17 May 2001, < http://www.idsa.com/consumersurvey2001.html > (accessed 17 December 2003).

12. National Institute on Media and the Family, "Sixth Annual Video and Computer Game Report Card," 13 December 2001, < http://www.mediafamily.org/research/report_vgrc_2001-2.shtml > (accessed 17 December 2003).

13. "It's more than a Game," *Hobart Mercury (Australia)*, 23 June 2001.

14. Ibid.

15. *Fortune*, 6 July 1998.

Chapter 2

1. This fact may make readers wonder if gender explains the findings of this study better than game playing experience; we wondered that too. So we ran regression analysis on all of the variables in this study controlling for gender and found the patterns to still be consistent with what we have presented here.

2. Steven Poole, "Are We Losing Our Grip on Reality?" *Sunday Times* (London), 11 May 2003.

3. Kimberly M. Thompson and Kevin Haninger, "Violence in E-Rated Video Games," *Journal of the American Medical Association* 286, no. 5 (August 1, 2001): 591–598.

4. Studies that show a statistically significant correlation between game playing and aggressive behavior include: D.D. Buchman, J. B. Funk, "Video Game Controversies," *Pediatric Annals* 24, (1995): 91-94; E.F. Provenzo. *Video Kids: Making Sense of Nintendo* (Cambridge, MA: Harvard University Press, 1991); N. Schutte, J. Malouff, J. Post-Gorden, and A. Rodasta, "Effects of Playing Video Games on Children's Aggressive and Other Behaviors," *Journal of Applied Social Psychology* 18 (1988): 454-460. Studies that suggest that research really doesn't prove any correlation between game playing and aggressive behavior include: B. Gunter, *The Effects of Video Games on Children: The Myth*

Unmasked (Sheffield, UK: Sheffield Academic Press, 1998); J. Sanger, *Young Children, Videos and Computer Games* (New York: The Falmer Press, 1996). K. Durkin, "Computer Games, Their Effects on Young People: A Review," Sydney Australia: Office of Film & Literature Classification, 1995.

5. John Tierney, "Here Come the Alpha Pups," *New York Times*, 5 August 2001.

6. Nick Yee, "Gaming with Romantic Partners: A Survey of *Everquest* players," 2001, < http://www.nickyee.com/eqt/partner. html > (accessed 17 December 2003).

Chapter 3

1. By one estimate, typical American teens will have played ten thousand hours of digital games by the time they begin their careers. Marc Prensky, *Digital Game-Based Learning* (New York: McGraw Hill, 2001).

2. Art Dudley, "How We Review," *Listener* (Summer 1995), 31.

3. Rich Handley, "Modeling and Simulation: Hollywood Fulfills Military Needs; Computer Game Developers and Movie Studios Are Breathing New Life into Military Training and Recruiting Efforts," *Advanced Imaging*, 1 March 2003.

Chapter 4

1. Catherine Bush, "How to Multitask," *New York Times*, 8 April 2001.

2. For examples, see Web sites such as < http://www.evolvinglogic.com >.

3. The game can be downloaded at < http://www.americasarmy. com >; recruiting language from U.S. Army, "GoArmy.com," 17 December 2003, < http://www.goarmy.com/index05.htm# > (accessed 17 December 2003).

Chapter 5

1. V. H. Vroom and P. W. Yetton, *Leadership and Decision Making* (Pittsburgh: University of Pittsburgh Press, 1973). See also V. H. Vroom and A. G. Jago, *The New Leadership: Managing Participation in Organizations* (Englewood Cliffs, NJ: Prentice Hall, 1988).

Chapter 6

1. "National Survey Finds: Financially Speaking, Many Single Young Women Show Signs of 'Carrie Bradshaw Syndrome'," *PR Newswire*, 1 May 2001.
2. Ibid.
3. Marc Prensky, "Reaching Younger Workers Who Think Differently," January 1998, < http://www.marcprensky.com/writing/Prensky%20-%20Twitch%20Speed.html > (accessed 14 April 2004).
4. American Savings Education Council, "1999 Youth & Money Survey," < http://www.asec.org/youthsurvey.pdf > (accessed 14 April 2004).
5. Obe Hostetter, "Video Games: The Necessity of Incorporating Video Games as Part of Constructivist Learning," 1 December 2002, < http://www.game-research.com/art_games_contructivist.asp > (accessed 17 December 2003).
6. Neopets, "About Us," < http://info.neopets.com/aboutus/ > (accessed 27 January 2004).

Chapter 7

1. John Leland, "Bigger, Faster, Bolder, Weirder," *New York Times*, 27 October 2002.

Chapter 8

1. New York City Councilman Eric Gioia (D-Queens) at a City Hall press conference, quoted in Eilis Quinn, "Video Games Not Kid Stuff, Parents Told," *New York Daily News*, 9 December 2002.
2. Dr. Carol Nati, a psychiatrist at Cook Children's Medical Center, quoted inChris Vaughn, "Forum Urges Protecting Youths from Media Violence," *Fort Worth Star Telegram*, 21 April 2002.
3. Jon C. Coates, Halifax, Nova Scotia, "Don't Celebrate Sales of Video Games," letter to the editor, *Halifax Daily News*, 31 December 2002.
4. David Lang, 18, of Northridge, California, quoted in James Nash, "Game Over for Cyber Cafes?" *LA Daily News*, 30 March 2003.

Index

ambition, gamers and, 184
attention management. *See also*
  concentration; multitasking
  back-of-mind/front-of-mind, 89
  video games and, 63–64
Atari, 8, 10, 30

baby boomers, 16
  attitude toward video games,
    6, 20–21, 174
  generation gap and, 6–8, 19–20,
    27–28, 174
  loyalty to organization, 82–86
  organizational models and,
    156–157
  risk and, 134, 135–136
  socialization of, 112–117
  trial-and-error learning and,
    145
business behavior, change in,
  27–28

business model. *See*
  organizations

Card, Orson Scott, 69
cognitive skills
  gamers and, 35, 155–165, 177
  multitasking and, 86–89
competition, gamers' attitude
  about, 12, 81–84
computer games, 7
concentration. *See also* attention
  management, multitasking
  boomers versus gamers, 86–89
confidence, and gamers, 79–81,
  95–96, 150
coworkers, gamers' attitude
  toward, 121–122
culture
  change in corporate, 129–132
  defined, 177
  shift, 175–176

About the Authors

John C. Beck is President of the North Star Leadership Group, Senior Research Fellow at the Annenberg Center of the Digital Future, University of Southern California, and a member of the Monitor Executive Development Faculty Network. His teaching and research focus on strategy, globalization, and leadership. Dr. Beck currently teaches at the Ivey School of Business and Thunderbird, the American Graduate School of International Management; he has also taught at Harvard, Dartmouth, and Northwestern's Kellogg School of Management. He brings to the analysis of videogames and business not only his perspective as a scholar and strategist, but also particular insight into games' power at attention management; Dr. Beck co-authored the Harvard Business School Press title *The Attention Economy*, named one of the year's ten best business books by Amazon, the American Library Association, and others. He can be reached at jbeck@northstarleadership.com.

Mitchell Wade analyzes the business impact of digital games from a very practical point of view: twenty years of experience helping companies use information to get results from key people. Most recently, his novel approach moved senior executives of an industry-defining firm to strengthen their own leadership and coach their teams to greater success. Mr. Wade has explored the link between information and action in such demanding settings as the pre-eminent think tank RAND, where he innovated in both communications and strategic-planning. He has worked with nonprofits, start-ups, government agencies, and members of the *Fortune* 500. His clients have included Google, Inc., Charles Schwab, Accenture, and the White House science advisor. He has also taught thought leaders and researchers at, for example, Harvard, the Claremont Colleges, and Cedars Sinai Medical Center to use information more effectively. He understands the connection between personal drives and organizational results; with John Beck, he wrote the leadership study *DoCoMo* (American Management Association, 2002), summarized by the *Boston Globe* as "that rarest of business books, one that reaches beyond business logic to reveal what comes from the heart." He can be reached at mitchellwade@gotgamebook.com.